Harry Worsfold
(1839–1939)
'The life and times of a gentleman of Surrey'

CW00553298

Harry Worsfold
(1839–1939)
'The life and times of a gentleman of Surrey'

JANET HILDERLEY

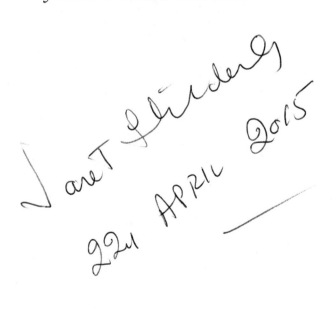

THE *Alpha* PRESS

BRIGHTON • CHICAGO • TORONTO

2 4 6 8 10 9 7 5 3 1

First published 2015 in Great Britain in the United Kingdom by
THE ALPHA PRESS
PO Box 139   Eastbourne BN24 9BP

and in the United States of America by
THE ALPHA PRESS
Independent Publishers Group
814 North Franklin Street, Chicago, IL 60610

and in Canada by
THE ALPHA PRESS (CANADA)

British Library Cataloguing in Publication Data
A CIP catalogue record for this book is available from the British Library.

Library of Congress Cataloging-in-Publication Data
Applied for.

ISBN 978-1-898595-62-5 (pbk)

Typeset & designed by The Alpha Press, Brighton & Eastbourne.
Printed by TJ International, Padstow, Cornwall.

Contents

Acknowledgements

My thanks go to the librarians of:

Guildford Public Library
Guildford Institute Library

Steve Mitchell of Radstone Computer Services

The staffs of:
Brooklands Museum
Godalming Museum
Guildford Museum
The Lightbox (The Woking story)
The National Trust
Royal Horticultural Society
Send and Ripley History Society
Surrey Advertiser
Surrey History Centre

AND
Cobham Conservation and Heritage Trust

Marjorie Williams and the staff of
Surrey Archaeological Society

Pam Bowles of Horsley Countryside Preservation Society

Daphne McFarlane for checking the manuscript and giving
support and encouragement.

CHAPTER ONE

Date of Birth, about 1840

Beginnings and Change

It is the 2nd of February 1939. Grandfather Worsfold goes for his after-dinner "lie-down". In sixteen days' time he will be one hundred years old. Harry falls asleep thinking of his party. In the kitchen, a hundred rock cakes bake in the kitchen range. On top of each one, a glacé cherry glistens. As the slate clock on the mantle chimes three, his daughter Florence climbs the stairs. There is no sound except for the bedroom door creaking open, then she calls out, "Father's gone!" Mrs Hilderley junior, his granddaughter-in-law, exclaims, "They'll be no good now, not for a funeral, not with those cherries on top." A week later, mourners mutter to each other, "are we to face another war?"

No birth certificate was found for Harry Worsfold. His death certificate states *date of birth about 1840*. However, he was baptised on 20th March 1842 in St John the Evangelist, Stoke. His marriage license shows him as Henry Worsfold, labourer of Stoke-next-Guildford, marrying Hannah Sale, a pretty, twenty-three-year-old Ripley girl. The certificate is dated 2nd January 1864. Harry's age is given as twenty-two. The certificate is witnessed by his father, George, and Hannah's father, John Sale. Both men were labourers. No mention is made of Harry's bride possessing one eye. The young couple signed the certificate together, firmly. In 1829, George Worsfold had married Elizabeth Hopkins in the same church.

The ceremony took place in St Mary Magdalene, a small chapel of ease, a Norman place built about 1160. In those days,

it was a Catholic priest who welcomed young brides. Certainly
the Norman presence was strong in the area. The King came to
nearby Guildford at Christmas, often dressed in swansdown,
lavishly entertaining in the Castle. Beforehand, his steward
visited the merchants in the High Street, buying new wine from
Bordeaux.

The three million souls living in England enjoyed a particularly warm spell during the years of hated King John, but they
found some consolation in the old religion. He was a distant
figure, but the Bishop of Winchester was not. During the year
1200, the black-habited monks of the Augustinian order, on his
orders, built a priory close to the River Wey in the parish of
Send. St Mary Magdalene, in the smaller village of Ripley, was
completed in a simpler style. It offered hospitality to wayfarers,
and comfort to the sick and the dying.

Many years later, in September 1852, the young Harry
Worsfold tolled the bell of St Mary's for three hours. Far away
in St Paul's Cathedral, the funeral was taking place of the Duke
of Wellington. In 1861, three years before his marriage, Harry
Worsfold tolled the bell again, this time to announce a queen's
grief. Her prince had died, leaving Victoria to mourn his
passing for forty long years. The final time Harry rang the bell
would be in 1918, telling folk that the Great War was over. The
women of Ripley cried for husbands and sons whom they would
see no more, many of them little more than boys. The lights had
gone out all over Europe, but Harry said, "Things are getting
better for us ordinary folk."

After the War, what remained of the young tried forgetting
its horrors and entered into a state of mad gaiety. This was
followed by depression, but Harry was right. Working at
factory bench and on the land during the war years, women
refused to return to being mere chattels. Now children stayed
on at school until they were thirteen years of age. In summertime, few small boys went shoeless as Harry had. He thought
modern boys "too mouthy and life dull for youngsters now", no

carriages now came rushing down the Portsmouth Road nor coachmen swore as boys threw stones at the passengers. Harry considered it to be a dull pastime calling out rude remarks to the newfangled automobile drivers or cyclists.

The hunt still rampaged across the countryside, but people were more aware that animals too felt pain. His grandson Charlie did not go out into the fields waving a worm held high on a stick to tempt a lark to swoop down and get caught for supper: *Take two dozen larks, clean and pluck. Cut off head and legs. Remove gizzards. Brush over with a well-beaten egg, dip the birds in nutmeg, breadcrumbs, then season and add a sprig of parsley. Roast in a baking-tin in a fairly hot oven. Baste the birds constantly else they will burn. Serve with good, meaty gravy. Dish will serve 6 to 8 persons. Allow one hour for cooking.*

Like many young children, Harry learned his letters at Sunday school. His younger siblings may have attended the Stoke Parochial School founded in 1856 *for affording a sound education to the children of the poor belonging to the parish at 2d a week. It is supported by yearly subscriptions and contributions, annual sermons being preached on its behalf.* Nevertheless, Harry's life remained one of ghosts and superstition, but he was not one of Bettesworth's illiterate peasants, unable to think and only reacting like some dumb animal. However, when he reached five years of age, his parents set him to work. There were other mouths to feed. At harvest time, he delivered his father's "fourses", or teas. A small boy was useful in helping to stack the harvest. "Many a time," he recalled, "I lay down between the stacks after I had done work and bid my time till I started reapin' again in the morning." The idea appealed to Charlie, but Flo said, "You would find it cold waking-up towards dawn."

"We did," said Harry. "But then as soon as you waked up, 'twas time to set to again."

There was no question of "sleeping-over" when he helped to feed the shire horses which pulled the flat barges along Sir Richard Weston's canal. Rumour had it that the Wey

Navigation nearly bankrupted him. In 1641, he sold to Sir Richard Onslow his hunting lodge at West Clandon, together with its thousand-acre estates. Sir Richard arrived at the turning point of the battle of Worcester. "Sorry, got lost," he told Cromwell. Angrily, the General called him *the Red Fox of Surrey*.

Sir Richard Weston's great-great-grandfather, also a Richard, was one of Henry VIII's favourites. Nevertheless, Henry beheaded his son for a so-called liaison with his Queen, Anne Boleyn. In 1525, Weston built a great mansion, Sutton Place, close to Oatlands Palace at Weybridge, where the King constructed a home for Anne of Cleves, his fourth and most unattractive wife. Despite disappointing her husband, she kept her head. His fifth wife, the young and beautiful Catherine Howard, also stayed at Oatlands. Her ghost haunts Hampton Court, crying out to her husband for mercy. Sutton Place is not a haunted palace or castle, but built in the style of a Tudor country mansion. It was surrounded by small manor houses and farms whose names are still remembered: Burchatt's, Stoke Park, and Abbot's Woods.

The great house stands in low-lying ground which the River Wey used to flood. Preserved in the house is the ruff of the beheaded Sir Thomas More, stained with his blood. In 1591, Henry VIII's daughter, Queen Elizabeth, came to stay at Sutton Place. Soon after her departure, the great hall burned down. It was not repaired until two hundred years later.

In 1635, Sir Richard submitted plans to Charles I. He wanted to improve the flow of the river. He cut, dug, and made a trench through the lands of his neighbour, Sir George Stoughton, Stoke's Lord of the Manor. The diarist John Aubrey commented that "Sir Richard's flowing river enabled six score acres of grounds to be flooded which was before most of it dry. The land next to the canal yielded two hundred loads of hay more per year." Sir Richard stated that a "hundred and fifty loads of my extraordinary hay sold at near three pounds a load".

At the beginning of the Civil War, as a Royalist and Roman

Catholic, Sir Richard's estates were seized and he fled abroad. Uninterested in politics, he petitioned to be allowed to return. Following Charles I's execution in 1649, Oatlands Palace was destroyed. Sir Richard began to build his canal's bridges and locks using the narrow red bricks collected from the debris of the Tudor palace.

Sir Richard Onslow, now a follower of the Puritan cause, must have watched fascinated as work commenced again on the canal. When he refused to sign Charles I's death warrant, Lord Cromwell advised him to spend more time with his family. Nine months after the work began on 7th May 1652, Sir Richard Weston died. Ten miles out of the fourteen had been completed. However, the canal remained subject to confrontations and squabbles. In 1651, his son George engaged a partner, James Pitson, a major in Cromwell's army. By 1653, the Wey Navigation Canal was finished. The waterways of England had always been used to move goods, and now the Wey Navigation's barges carried easily cargoes, such as corn, flour, timber, coal, chalk, bark for tanning, rags for paper making, barrel hoops, ironwork, sugar, groceries, and gunpowder, from Guildford to London's docks. Usually, two horses in tandem pulled the barges, often Clydesdales. These were stabled at either Newark Mill or Worsfold Gates at Send. Something of a "sylvan scene", the River Wey flows through the Gates. The name is thought to have come from one of the original labourers who, in 1671, made a claim for £60 *for work done repairing the banks at a rate of 5/- a week.*

The canal did not immediately decline in competition to the railways. At the time when Harry was a boy, it had had many owners and was managed by William Stevens, who named his new barge *Perseverance*. His family followed in the old canal traditions. Harry watched fascinated as women sat knitting in the barges, jumping up as the lock gates came into sight and grabbing a crowbar. The paddles on the two sets of gates had to be levered up so that the peg could be put in place. The peg-

and-hole method was easy when the water pressure on the paddle was low, but hard work when it was normal. Once the water returned to the right level, they returned to their work, hoping to sell the goods at Guildford's cattle market or the county fair.

Guildford found it difficult to site wharves for the barges to unload, especially as they often carried gunpowder. However, Stoke-next-Guildford had room for a large wharf. In 1654, the people of Guildford signed a petition complaining that the undertakers (canal managers) should find a place to land commodities within Guildford: "It is manifest that they intend to take the whole business and accommodation from the said town of Guildford to Stoke and other places to the impoverishment of the said town."

As a boy, Harry helped lift the cargoes out of the barges on to Dapdune Wharf. On leaving the canal, he wandered into Woodbridge Road. This area of Stoke still retains the feel of a village and, in Harry's day, prosperous Londoners thought they were buying a place in the country. Making his way to Joseph Street, he would pass two of the oldest cottages in Stoke: no. 35-37, part-built in the 15th century and thatched. Nearby stand nos. 9, 10, and 11, belonging to the 16th and 17th centuries. He wondered about the residents of these properties. Little documentation exists to explain who they were. As in every corner of Surrey, the presence of the Onslows is felt. Along the street, he would see a Tudor "farmhouse". It is one of the oldest in the district and, sadly, again few documentary sources exist, but it is known that the house was owned by Mr Middleton Onslow in the 18th century.

Acquaintances of the Worsfolds, the Smallpieces were a Surrey family of long standing. Evidence of this is shown when they were mentioned, in 1570, in the deeds of Watford Farm House of Stoke: "John Smallpiece of Guildford, clothier, conveyed to George Parvis of Watford, Stoke, yeoman, a half acre in Stoke Field next to Parsonage Path."

Harry thought his family origins were Germanic. Later research considers they may have been called Von Varsfeld, coming to England as mercenaries to fight for Edward IV in the 15th century. Since then, the name Worsfold has become synonymous with the Surrey countryside. Some authorities believe the name comes from the site of a deserted Surrey village or hamlet. During the 14th century, many villages were cleared to make room for sheep farming. Others say it comes from the Old English "werf", meaning draught cattle, and fields, called "felds".

Harry's own life possessed its excitements. He told tales of old Surrey but, of course, they are impossible to verify after all this time. He remembered a few occasions when, as a boy, he crawled through a hedge at midnight to open a farm gate. Black-hooded figures on horseback passed silently through, dragging kegs of brandy or "baccy" behind them – or, more likely, people who wished to escape unnoticed to the continent. Portsmouth was less than fifty miles down the road, and it was a straight run to London. Gertrude Jekyll talks in *Old West Surrey* of a new squire being informed that "there was a run last night, sir, and I've marked four." His rector told him, "If you wish to live in peace with your neighbours you had better fall in with the custom of the country."

No strong hand clasped Harry's shoulder. Young as he was, twenty years before he would have been strung up in Guildford's Tunsgate. Fortunately for him, execution by hanging was abolished in 1836, except for murder. Nevertheless, he would have done time. The town's House of Correction being closed, Harry would have spent a period in Surrey County Gaol, otherwise known as the New Gaol. The criminal classes referred to it as "Horsemonger Lane", after the thoroughfare in Wandsworth in which it stood. On release, the boy would have drifted into London and joined the flotsam and jetsam of the capital's underworld.

In 1849, Dickens wrote his famous letter condemning public

hangings. The behaviour of the crowd shook him. When Harry was about eleven years of age, his parents took him as a special treat to Albury, to see the murderer John Keene hung. As the executioner tied the rope around the man's neck, he cried out, "I didn't do it! I didn't throw the little boy down the well!"

Sometime in 1850, a twenty-five-year-old single mother, Jane Broomer, married John Keene. Subsequently, she bore his baby. In January 1852, Jane told her mother that Keene had thrown Charlie, her illegitimate son, a toddler, down Warren Well on Albury Heath. Hearing rumours, Superintendent Josiah Ridley of Guildford police called on the Keenes. Jane was alone. She told him, "I know what you've come about – it's my husband having killed Charlie." Keene later denied the murder, saying, "I never put him in the water."

The well digger William Edsor climbed down to the bottom of Warren Well and found the body of the toddler. Ridley accused the couple of his murder. On 22nd March 1852, they were tried. Jane was found innocent; Keene convicted. He was hung before a lynch mob of several thousand, angered by the brutal murder of the child.

One of Harry's older brothers applied for the position of hangman. Sadly for him, the waiting list was too long. In old age, Harry said his youthful experiences helped to make him a successful parish constable. He boasted, "I am the last of the parish constables." Harry also reminded his family he had been butler to the 1st Earl of Lovelace, the man who married Ada, the computer innovator and Lord Byron's daughter, but the 1911 census shows Harry, in his seventies, as "road mender for Surrey County Council". A man who became something of a folk hero, known for his prodigious memory and intelligence, never mentioned that.

Harry preferred to work and rely on his own meagre savings rather than be means-tested and paid a pension by the state. He kept his savings: £5 note by £5 note, hidden behind the paintings hanging on the walls of his cottage. Fortunately, he never had to rely on his children, and all twelve grew into healthy adults. He knew that at least one of them would be able to care for Hannah and himself, if necessary, but *not* if he "disappeared into foolishness" – then there was only one place for him: Stoke's lunatic asylum, Leapale House, in Mad House Lane. Nobody knew when it took on this role, but it was thought it stood on the site of a medieval leper colony. The house was licensed to care for twenty insane persons, both female and male.

When Harry was an infant, the asylum was run by a Dr Sells, nicknamed "Butcher Sells". It was listed as a lunatic asylum until the 1870s, but in the 1880s, an engineering company took over and the house became the subject of many tales, usually told by an old woman "with a mouth like the village pump".

As Harry began earning his own living, he feared a bad harvest. Like most of his sort, he dreaded going into the Union Workhouse at Slyfield, which he assumed he would have to do in order to avoid starving in the gutter. He did not know of the minutes of the Board of Guardians dated 1st May 1836, which stated *no relief be given to any able bodied paupers in the Guildford district of the Union from and after the 4th June*. It was assumed that a young man would be able to find work. Like many young people, if disaster had struck, he would probably have joined the two million people living in London.

There was assistance for his sisters if they became house-keepers. In 1767, Mr James Price left £400 for the benefit of poor housekeepers not eligible for parish relief. His nephew, Dr James Price, a Fellow of the Royal Society, added a further £800 to the charity. He committed suicide following his claims of being able to transmute mercury and silver into gold. The Society insisted he performed his experiments in front of a group of qualified chemists. On 3rd August 1783, he was prepared to do so, but fell dead at his audience's feet.

If Harry's mother ever fell on hard times, as a respectable widow she would be eligible to enter Parsons Almshouse in Stoke Road as one of the six poor "sisters" from Stoke or

Worplesdon. The memorial on the front of the building reads "This Hospital was Given and Established in the year 1796 by William and Henry Parson of this parish." They were successful drapers in Guildford. The hospital is constructed in the Georgian style with Gothic windows. Now traffic roars out of Guildford towards London, but when the almshouse was built, the site was isolated. In the centre of its roof sits a cupola with a clock and bell waiting to take action.

The rules stated that the widows must attend services at Stoke parish church, St John the Evangelist, twice on Sundays, and in their own chapel on Wednesdays and Fridays. The almshouse's gates were open from 7 a.m. to 8 p.m. in the summer, and from 8 a.m. to 6 p.m. in the winter. The inmates received 4/- a week, the matron 5/-, and all of them would be given a blue gown of broadcloth every two years. They had two rooms each and were provided with free fuel for their fires.

The Parson brothers lay in the churchyard. As the sisters listened to the rector's sermon, they could observe two brass memorials placed on the north wall of the church: "In memory of Henry Parson and draper of Guildford who departed this life in . . . 1791 aged 62 years. Also, in memory of William Parson, later mercer and draper of Guildford and brother to Henry Parson who departed this life in . . . 1799 aged 73 years."

If the women's minds wandered, they could consider the problem of the church's foundations – were they Saxon? Nobody knows for certain. Certainly the nave and south chapel belong to the early 14ᵗʰ century. The residents could also contemplate why the rector lived in a parsonage and not a rectory. The "sisters" could also study an east window in the Stoughton Chapel. Lord of the Manor Mr Nathaniel Hillier collected the glass during the 17ᵗʰ century. Pevsner commented that "the vigorous east window – an unusual design." The Hilliers were Methodists and shrewd merchants dealing in fine textiles. They were also members of the city's premier livery company, the Mercers Company.

The family business had diversified into bookselling and printing. The son of a printer, bookseller, and former Mayor of Guildford, John Russell painted the couple's portraits. Their pastel likenesses observe visitors in Clandon Park's morning room. John Russell, a deeply spiritual man and a Methodist, discussed religion with George Onslow, the 1st Earl and friend of royalty. He can be seen in the Speaker's Parlour dressed in the Windsor uniform only worn by those closest to King George III.

The Hillier's second daughter, Susannah, married Thomas Cranley Onslow in 1812, second son of the 2nd Earl of Onslow. Nathaniel Hillier's estates passed to Susannah. They were the great-grandparents of William Hillier, the 4th Earl of Onslow, who at the age of seventeen, in 1870, inherited Clandon Park as well as Stoke Park, which his great-grandfather Nathaniel Hillier had bought sixty-nine years before. The young man decided he must sell Stoke Park and put all his energies into saving Clandon Park.

As much as Harry distrusted London and its ways, Guildford and its environment owed much to a wealthy City merchant, Alderman Smith. A childless widower, he left his wealth to be used for charitable purposes. The Henry Smith Charity purchased land in Guildford High Street, which included the town mills and the Poyle estates around Stoke. In 1650, the trustees allotted the rents so that "the rents and profits should be received by the mayor and approved men . . . and equally divided among the poor." In that year, the trustees allotted the rents from Henry Smith's Warbleton estates in East Sussex. Stoke-next-Guildford received £12 to be given to aged, poor, and infirm persons.

As close as the capital was, Harry rarely visited London. On one occasion, he came to the capital to witness the funeral of the "Grand Old Man", Prime Minister Gladstone. He thought London dirty, crowded, and unsanitary. He told his grandson Charlie, "I remember stories of the cholera which swept through

the East End in 1866. They said even the Prime Minister's wife
came to nurse the dying. The undertakers ordered hearses to
carry twelve coffins at a time. That was caused by water."

"Dirty water, grandpa," corrected Charlie.

Harry told his family that, in 1866, two cases of cholera were
reported in Ripley. One resulted in a death. The victim was a
John Smith, who was buried on 27th July. His entry in the parish
register describes him as a "stranger who died in a 'van on Ripley
Green".

Country people drank small beer rather than water. They
used it for washing and, if necessary, cooking. Harry remained
wary of it even when it came out of a tap. Many households
brewed their own beer; for instance, Guildford House possessed
a brewhouse. Mr George Smallpiece owned Malthouse Cottages
close to Stoke Mill on the Wey Navigation Canal. Later, the
cottages became the Row Barge Inn, and the bargemen lived in
Malthouse Lane. Such was the consumption of alcohol in
Guildford and its surrounds that, in 1880, the 4th Earl of
Onslow laid the foundation stone for the Royal Arms
Temperance Hotel. It was not a success, and subsequently
became the Mechanics Institute "for the promotion of useful
knowledge among the working classes." The building is now
the Guildford Institute. Its magnificent library is used by
students up and down the country.

In fact, it was the government that encouraged beer drinking
rather than cheap spirits, such as gin, which had blighted the
lives of the poor in the 18th century. Guildford's Chertsey Street
provided numerous inns, public houses, and beer shops to cater
for its growing population, together with licentious soldiery
and seamen who travelled to and from Portsmouth.

If Harry walked along the street today, he would recognize
the Stoke, Prince Albert, and the Spread Eagle. However, he
would not find a greengrocer with a beer shop attached. Should
he go further along into Woodbridge Road he would come
across the Drummond Arms, built in 1850 for West Surrey's

Henry Drummond, MP, banker, owner of Albury Park, and supporter of the Catholic Apostolic Church.

Harry never visited Albury. He did not wish to be reminded of the hanging he had witnessed. Miss Jekyll would have known of Albury Park and the strange tale of this transplanted village. As she approached it from the Surrey hills, she would have seen the tall chimneys rising above the few cottages standing either side of the High Street. In the 17th century, Albury Park belonged to the family of the Duke of Norfolk. The cottages clustered around the mansion, the village green, and a church built in Saxon times. The diarist John Evelyn laid out the gardens for the Howards. William Cobbett described them, in 1822, as *the prettiest . . . that I ever saw in England.* There were links with royalty. Towards the end of the 17th century, the 1st Earl of Aylesford, solicitor-general to Charles II, owned the place.

Local rumours say that George III held his coronation banquet in Albury Park. At the end of the 18th century, the mansion changed ownership again and became the property of a wealthy naval captain, William Clement Finch. He disliked the closeness of the cottagers to his mansion, and enclosed the green, incorporating part of the churchyard into its grounds. Finch harassed the villagers so much that they moved into nearby Weston Street.

In 1819, Henry Drummond purchased Albury Park. He found the old church, partly built by the Saxons, in need of repair. Twenty years later, Drummond applied to the Bishop of Winchester to close it, and built a new church at Weston where the present village stands. He commissioned the multifaceted chimneys described by Eric Parker as *tall and graceful, of red brick, shaped and moulded in ingenious spirals, with patterned sides and columns, and crowsteps and other ornaments and uses. You could not guess all that village chimneys can be, until you have seen Albury.*

It was at Albury Park that the Scottish preacher Edward Irving started the Catholic Apostolic Church, a complex set of beliefs, for those who followed the Nicene Creed. Irvine was keenly supported by Thomas Carlyle. Henry Drummond was another enthusiastic follower. At a cost of £16,000, he built a church for the "Irvinites". The last "Apostle" died in 1901. It is closed to the public and waits patiently, tucked away behind trees, for the Second Coming of Christ.

In the towns, by the middle of the 19th century, Nonconformist beliefs attracted the educated lower-middle classes. Harry rarely attended Matins, "that was for 'toffs'." Instead, he went to Evening Prayers. However, the growing interest in Nonconformity led to a Methodist church being erected on the corner of Woodbridge Road and North Street in the 1840s.

Next door, the minister built his manse. This not only provided shelter for him, but also stabling for his horse. Banker William Haydon donated a barrel organ to play hymns, which was worked by a blacksmith from Stoke Fields. In 1853, a Congregational chapel was erected on the corner of Leapale Road and North Street. Due to the energy of its minister, the Rev'd John Hart, it was built in less than six months.

Harry remained loyal to the Church of England even though he said "the quality only attend to be seen and their women to observe the bonnets of the other women." By this time, Guildford was already encroaching on Stoke, and in 1861, the County and Borough Halls appeared opposite the Congregational Chapel.

Even though the lives of the poor at this time were slowly improving, the old social divisions remained. Miss Gertrude Jekyll sympathized with them. She spent much of her childhood chatting to "cottagers". When Harry grew up, he would hear of the activities of Miss Jekyll. She would influence Surrey life and his son-in-law, George. However, as a small boy, Harry would have known nothing of the five-year-old girl suffering from myopia who came to live with her dog Crum in the village of Bramley, close to Albury and Godalming.

Captain Jekyll rented Bramley House from Lady Egremont of Petworth.

The village was in poor farming country, a long way away from Gertrude's birthplace, 40 Grafton Street, close to the Crown Estate of Berkeley Square. Her family left behind them "Gunter's Tearooms" with its special blackcurrant ice creams and grand neighbours such as the Rothschilds, Grosvenors, and the ghost at number 50 – a house once owned by Prime Minister Sir George Canning. Legend says it is the spirit of a young woman who, for love, threw herself out of an attic bedroom window. Canning reported hearing strange noises in the night, and moved. Lord Lyttleton fired a shotgun at the apparition. An unfortunate young maid saw something terrible and went mad. When the owners failed to pay the rates, Westminster Council let them off due to the house's reputation.

The Jekylls must have found their neighbours non-intellectual country gentry. Gertrude's father, a retired captain of the Grenadier Guards, a nervous, intellectual invalid unable to stand noise, delighted in the quiet. His elder daughter, Carolyn, had married and lived in Venice. The boys had gone away to school. It left only Gertrude and baby Herbert in the nursery.

Captain Jekyll continued to collect Etruscan vases and enjoy his life-sized casts of Venus de Milo, but his wife, the former Julia Hammersley, an aristocrat and daughter of a banker, could not have appreciated rural life. Mrs Jekyll was artistic, musical, an expert on Bach, and taught by Felix Mendelssohn to play the piano. The couple left Gertrude to wander through the countryside, alone, with her dog. She got to know the cottagers and their ways. This way, the young girl discovered old Surrey and called it "an enchanted land". She came across a pond whose great poplars dangled their branches into its waters. Hidden in the tangle of undergrowth, moorhens built their nests.

Gertrude often wandered down the lane going into Bramley. When she heard the wheels of the carrier's cart and saw his dogs pulling it along, panting heavily, she prepared to spring aboard.

As she settled down, Gertrude counted the number of parcels
being brought from Guildford station. Otherwise, she watched
the strong horses pulling the fishmonger's brightly-painted
yellow van crammed full of fish. They had been caught early in
the morning, and travelled from the seaports, arriving by
midday in the market towns. The fishmonger would call out,
"Oysters three a penny, or four if still alive." At the end of the
day, his fish would be displayed on London dinner plates.

Crum would run barking behind the smaller carts, drawn by
two or four Newfoundland dogs. In the morning and early
evening, Gertrude listened for the postman's horn. For a penny,
you could buy a stamp, and the letter you gave the postman
would arrive the next day. Most of all, Gertrude remembered
the old corn mill, its lichen roof and grapevine clambering over
its mellowing walls which were mentioned in the Domesday
Book and, in the 17ᵗʰ century, leased to a Jasper Shrubb. He too
would have heard doves cooing in the dovecot; perhaps even the
sound of medieval music drifting from the church. As everybody
knew, nobody was there.

One person's arrival caused great excitement. It was the
tinker, always alone. He brought goods, such as buttons, pegs,
wooden dolls, etc., and new wonders like envelopes, found for
the first time at the Great Exhibition. News came slowly to the
countryside in those days, but the tinker brought tales from the
great world. He talked of kings and queens, of revolutions, of
marvellous "Puffing Billies" which steamed their way along
with no help from horses. They went through the countryside
at thirty miles per hour. He spoke of factories which housed
machines that hammered away day and night, replacing men.
Most of all, the tinker brought news of working men who
demanded their rights. He spoke of revolutions and wars.

Captain Jekyll would have read about the Crimean War in
The Times or *The Telegraph*. They were not for the likes of Harry,
but he knew of young men enlisting in the Surreys. They were
stationed in the barracks at Stoke-next-Guildford. As old men,

they told tales, as did Surrey labourer "Old Bettesworth", who enlisted at Alton when he was sixteen and served a year and eight months, two winters and a summer, in the Crimea, before Sebastopol. He talked of the Kertch, the Black Sea, and the Dardanelles:

Sixteen of us in one o' they little tents. We had a blanket and a waterproof sheet – not the first winter, though; and boots that come up to your thigh, big enough to get into with your shoes on. I'ved bin out on duty forty-eight hours at a stretch, then march back three mile to camp . . . and then some of us had to march another seven mile to fetch biscuit from sea . . . sometime the biscuit was dry; and then again you on'y git some as had bin trod to death by mules or camels . . . but there was plenty o' rum; good rum too, better'n what you gits about here. The men sometimes went weeks together without getting any pay, 6d a day – 4/2d. Greek coffee was provided. The dead were buried in their kit . . . we weren't allowed no plunder. You never saw no coffins.

The only coffin Bettesworth saw was Lord Raglan's: "That was a funeral! Seven miles long . . . ."

In 1853, following the Crimean War, the powers-that-be decided Guildford would become a garrison town. The town residents, forceful as always, had other ideas. The town of Aldershot was chosen in 1854, but the Stoughton Barracks were duly completed in 1876, close to the River Wey and bounding the Friary Breweries. Guildford had always been a military town.

As a young lady, Miss Jekyll would have attended balls in the town and danced with the young officers. When he was an old man, Harry sang to his grandson, "Charlie, its Tommy this and Tommy that, and Tommy how's your soul? But it's the thin red line of 'eroes when the drums begin to roll." He had heard tales of Miss Nightingale, naming one of his daughters Florence after her. She too possessed a caring nature.

Harry never went to war, but during the seventies' agricultural depression, two of his brothers joined the "Surreys". A year before, the recently-widowed new colonel of the 2nd Royal

Surrey Militia and Lord Lieutenant of the county of Surrey, the
1st Earl of Lovelace, established the officers' mess in the White
Hart Hotel at the top of Guildford. In a population of about
8,000, he billeted twenty officers and 1,000 men around the
town.

As usual on 5th November, the shopkeepers closed their businesses. Early in the evening, a group of masked men marched
up Guildford's High Street and lit a bonfire outside Holy
Trinity, the parish church. A mob gathered. As the bonfire
burned down, the "Guys" led the crowd to plunder the town. A
local carpenter, John Mason, declared, "Guildford boys were
born with the uncontrollable habit of celebrating bonfire night
the way their fathers had done." Ever since 1605, Guildford had
celebrated King James I's escape from being blown apart by
Guy Fawkes. However, following the French Revolution, the
citizens feared the mob and banned bonfires and public cele-
brations. On Guy Fawkes Night the Guys would mass on the
edge of the town from daybreak, wearing masks or strange
disguises and armed with clubs and lighted torches. As night
fell, they entered the town to assault those who had crossed them
during the year, or loot or damage property, and burned fires in
the middle of the High Street. The riots caused the death of two
police officers. A young architect, Henry Peak, newly arrived in
Guildford, described in his diary how the riots took hold that
night. The town's police force consisted of three officers and
several unreliable special constables. The army were called out
to help, but they took time to arrive. The men were scattered
around the town. The sound of the Guy Riots' rallying call,
"Phillahoo Muster", continued to be heard until a forceful
mayor, P. W. Jacob, took office in 1865, and the riots had halted
by 1870.

The Mayor had needed the help of the army to quell the riots.
However, being so close to London, many of the great and
powerful lived locally and objected to the riots: Ockham Park,
Loseley Park, Sutton Place, Polesden Lacey, Hatchlands, and

Clandon Park, built in 1720 to entertain the Prince Regent. Queen Victoria visited Claremont at Esher often. It had belonged to her Uncle Leopold, the King of the Belgians. Harry saw "the old lady" once; she was stepping out of her carriage: "I will never forget that smile."

The More-Molyneauxs of Loseley Park are still recovering from the visits of Queen Elizabeth I. Her Majesty arrived five times. Most of the house had been built during 1562–68 by Sir William More, using stones from Waverley Abbey. It has been described as "a noble dwelling of grey gables and spacious windows". In 1601, Anne, the wayward daughter of Sir George, the son of Sir William, ran away to marry the poet John Donne. Together they produced twelve children.

King James I also visited Loseley. Perhaps due to the family's influence, the King persuaded Donne into taking Anglican orders. On the death of Sir George, his grandson Sir Poynings More inherited Loseley and found himself in a difficult position. In 1642, the Civil War began. Poynings was member of Parliament for Haslemere and Guildford, and a man who had received several favours from Charles I, including being created a baron on 18th May 1642. He spoke against the execution of the King and kept a low profile during the Civil War, but was annoyed when he found His Majesty's soldiers draining his lake and poaching his carp.

On the death of the 2nd Baron, Sir William More, the title became extinct. The estate then passed to the late baronet's uncle, the Rev'd Nicholas More. It then went to his daughter, Margaret, who had married Sir Thomas Molyneux. Their son was given the Christian name of More, and the family became known as More-Molyneux.

More's son inherited the estates in 1760. He was a successful soldier, Colonel Thomas More-Molyneux, who possessed expensive tastes, and Loseley suffered. Fortunately, his sister Jane inherited the estate in 1776. She was of a more careful nature. In 1779, only half the mince pies were made before Christmas

Day because plums were so expensive. She waited until after Christmas Day, "thinking the price might fall". The 1st Earl of Lovelace may well have approved – he was descended from an Exeter grocer.

Harry's life would be lived in the shadow of these great people, but the 1860s brought him marriage, children, and becoming a part of Ripley life. For another Henry they brought a new way of life. On 16th February 1851, a nineteen-year-old boy left London and his home to come to work in Guildford. Henry Peak found a building boom in full swing. The character of the High Street was changing, and many new shops were being built. North Street was also developing. Mr Peak was to become Guildford's first Borough Architect and Surveyor, as well as its much loved mayor.

Ripley remained a busy little place, but part of the old world. Mr Martyr delivered his bread from a handcart pulled in front of him by a big dog. Rag-and-bone men pushed a two-wheel barrow, calling out, "Any old iron?" Fortunately for them, most of the shopkeepers possessed horse-drawn vehicles. In the yard of the old Talbot Inn, horses were changed within minutes, but the last London to Portsmouth mail coach had passed through Ripley in 1842, two years after the completion of the London to Southampton railway. However, private carriages, stage-coaches, and wagons continued to trundle through the village. Ripley folk maintain they hear the coachman blowing the stage's horn, and the Red Rover comes galloping down the High Street. It was a world which Harry and Hannah hoped would never change.

CHAPTER TWO

The 1850s and 1860s

A Time to Sow and a Time to Reap

By 1851, the family had left Stoke-next-Guildford and moved into Ripley. The village lies on the Portsmouth Road, halfway between Kingston and Guildford. At that time, it was a place of coaching inns, cricket, and sailors en route to overcrowded and filthy Portsmouth. It is said that even Lord Nelson stayed at the Talbot Inn.

The census shows that Harry's parents were born in Ripley. His fourteen-year-old brother George is an agricultural labourer born in the village. The rest of the children are listed as scholars: Emma, eleven, Henry, nine, Jane, seven, and Mary, four, were born in Stoke-next-Guildford, except for Mary, who was born in Ripley. Jane and Mary appeared in the village school's lists for 1847. Harry and Emma do not.

However, on Harry's tenth birthday, it was time for him to go out to work. He became a "buttons" (page) to Mrs Christina Trevenas, an officer's widow who lived with her son-in-law, retired Major Pitcairn Onslow, at Dunsborough Park, together with his wife and seven children: Arthur, Frances, William, Edith, Marion, Charlotte, and George Thorpe. They would remember young Harry with affection and become useful contacts for him in later life.

The great house was close to the Worsfold household at 90 High Street, just off the High Street, across the Green, hidden behind a row of lime trees. The house is first mentioned in the Court Baron of 1535: *a parcel of land called "Little Dunsborrowe"*.

Harry would have been a suitable child for Mrs Trevenas to employ. He was intelligent, presentable, and able to read and write. With his excellent memory and clear speaking voice, he could run errands for her, deliver messages, and post letters. However, when he began to work for Major Onslow, much more would have been expected of him, including rising at five in the morning, and cleaning the cinders out of the grates and sifting them. Boots left outside the bedroom doors must be cleaned before the wearers rose. Mrs Beeton stressed *much delicacy of treatment is required in cleaning ladies' boots, so as to make the leather look well-polished*. Wood must be chopped for the fire, which would be placed under the copper and lit. The maids would then carry the hot water up the backstairs so that the family could wash themselves. The oven fires too must be lit early in order for the family to eat their breakfast on time and have their coffee ground. Meanwhile, coal scuttles were being filled in order to keep the upstairs rooms warm.

Harry would don his livery whenever he was to appear in front of the family. One young boy described his outfit as consisting of a black silk top hat with a cockade, and box-calf leather boots, together with a suit in fine black cloth with yellow facings and three rows of black, silk-covered buttons – hence the nickname "buttons".

During the day, Harry cleaned knives, plates, and washed the glass. These must go to the table in the highest state of brilliance. He may have mounted a ladder and, with great care, polished the windows. Another morning task was trimming the lamps. Once a week, these had to be taken to pieces and thoroughly cleaned. Harry's outside duties included removing the milking pails from the scullery, kept indoors for cleanliness, and taking them to the cowman. On his return, he collected the vegetables for dinner from the head gardener. The little boy would have gone to his bed when the family had no more need of him. Major Onslow would have been taxed 10/6d for employing a page. Harry's remuneration would have been about £8 a year, which included board, lodging, and livery.

His parents must have been proud of him. Within a few years, Harry, with his manly good looks and well-turned legs, could become an indoor servant such as a footman, working under the watchful eye of the butler. The livery of the indoor servants emphasized their remoteness from rough labourers and also displayed their employer's wealth. In the old days, Harry could have been a running footman, ready for action should the carriage overturn or become stuck in mud. Often, the footman ran ahead to prepare the destination for the arrival of his employer.

With application and "keeping-his-place", Harry may indeed have reached the dizzy heights of becoming a butler himself! In 1880, *The Servants Practical Guide* comments that *it is not unknown for a butler to be so consumed with pride that the mistress . . . stands greatly in awe of him.*

A life in service was not to be. Harry considered it "not a job for a man". His brother George seems to have remained at home even though Sturt says (in *Memories of a Surrey Labourer*) that *fifty years ago, it was the custom for the lads on a farm to live in the farm-house. The day's work would be hard and thorough; but at the close of it there would be any amount of bread and bacon and plenty of home-brewed beer, and in the winter a sure drowsy place by the kitchen fire.*

During the 1850s, Harry's father remained an agricultural labourer, but became sexton to St Mary Magdalene, Ripley's parish church, and the church records show *26th December 1856, Worsfold, Sexton paid 10 shillings.* Entries appear throughout the fifties: *Worsfold cleaned paths, five shillings; cut hedges, two shillings; paid Worsfold's bill 1d. May 13th, 1857, Worsfold clearing and cutting hedges, two shillings; Worsfold cleaned paths, five shillings. December 27th, Sexton paid 10/1; Worsfold cleaned paths, five shillings. 1859, Mr Smallpiece paid insurance, five guineas.* Such a role brought the Worsfold family into the centre of village life, knowing what was going on where, when, and with whom.

It was work which remained at the centre of most villagers' lives, even as children. Few ordinary people could read or write, and certainly would not have been aware that on 16ᵗʰ October 1811, the National Society for Promoting Religious Education was formed. They may have envied Joshua Watson, a leader of the Society, his skills for making a comfortable living. He sold and bought wine. However, they would have listened in respectful silence as the Vicar reminded them that it was the will of God for the rich man to live in the castle and the poor man to stand at his gate.

Certainly for a woman, it was believed that children were a gift sent to her by the Almighty, as the nearest route to the workhouse was to run out of relatives. However, a mother may have felt He did not appreciate the problems of feeding a large family on less than 10/- a week, and every penny her children brought in was welcomed (the average weekly income of 2014 is approximately £440 per week).

Many women had at least thirteen children in as many years. The older children helped look after the younger ones. Most of them, from their earliest years, had jobs to do – making paper spills to light the fire, cutting old suits down for rag rugs, fetching the jug of milk from the farm before school, and collecting wood for the fire.

They were not paid for their tasks. One child asked for a birthday present. She was told "your present is on your feet." Another had her new boots bought out of her moneybox. Her parents said, "you can have the pennies left over."

Clothing for a village child was simple, no laces or velvet for them. Heavy boots with hooks and laces were worn by both sexes. The girls put on pinafores over their frocks, and the boys wore a cap, which had to be raised for greetings. Toys were simple – tops, hoops (iron for boys, wooden for girls), and glass "alleys" – the marble from the neck of Stansfield's lemonade bottles being in great demand. Village children enjoyed country activities: ferreting, egg collecting, or fishing for "tiddlers".

However, most of the middle classes agreed that Christianity was the first and chief thing to be taught to the poor, *according to the excellent Liturgy and Catechism provided by our Church*. By 1846, this philosophy had so prevailed up and down the country that Send and Ripley also began fundraising to build a suitable school.

Like many a Church of England clergyman, the Vicar of Ripley, the Rev'd Henry Albany Bowles, was an excellent fundraiser. First, he asked permission from the Church's patron, the reclusive 3rd Earl of Onslow, to be allowed to build a school on his glebe land next to the church. He also discussed the venture with his bishop, Charles Sumner, Bishop of Winchester and father-in-law of the formidable Mrs Mary Sumner, the founder of the Mothers' Union.

Towards the end of 1846, Rev'd Albany Bowles could relax. He had raised £180 by appealing to the comfortably-off of his parish. This was half the sum required. He was then in a position to ask the National Society for the rest, stressing the need for Christian education in Send and Ripley. Already, some of the poor children received basic instruction through local Dame Schools.

Many parents struggled to find money to pay a semi-illiterate woman to provide day care or give their small children a basic education consisting of arithmetic, spelling, and grammar. A study of Dame Schools in 1838, by the Royal Statistical Society, found that over half of them possessed inadequate facilities.

Apart from actively fundraising, Mr Albany Bowles asked the wives of the churchwardens and other ladies of note to form a Ladies' Visiting Committee. The purpose was to show an interest in the children and make sure the establishment was properly run. In another school at nearby Downside, a kindly lady made, with her own hands, red woollen capes as a Christmas present for every village girl. The lady was startled to be asked by one independent child, "Thank you kindly, ma'am. If it pleases, I would prefer green next year."

By 1847, the plans for the Send and Ripley National School were completed. It opened in the High Street, next to the church. The scholars' parents contributed to the Children's Pence, which demanded a pre-decimalisation 1d a week for each child. The pupils raised funds by selling crafts such as basket-making or sewing mats, etc. All these efforts went towards paying the teachers' salaries.

Among the first pupils of the Send and Ripley School was Harry's future bride, six-year-old Hannah (in the 1851 census, the surname is spelt Sail), and her eight-year-old brother Reuben. Their elder sister, twenty-year-old Harriet, appears in the census as unemployed. She is seen no more, and vanishes from the scene. Their father gives his occupation as a tanner-journeyman. Nearly twenty years later, he signed his daughter's marriage certificate as a labourer.

This census shows John Weight as the National Schoolmaster. He was followed, in 1852, by Thomas Marriott Berridge who, in 1860, became Principal of Ryde House School in the High Street. It was a private day and boarding school for boys, next to Mrs Gail's Seminary for Young Ladies in Elm Tree House, at the far end of the village, close to the gates of Ockham Park and opposite Bridgefoot Farm where Harry would work.

It was during the 1860s that Ripley began to develop its reputation for excellent private schools. Mr Berridge started his school in Ryde House at the London end of Ripley High Street. In 1893, Ripley Court Preparatory School appeared in Rose Lane. It was built on the site of a Queen Anne farmhouse and inn, both built about 1730. The Turnpike Act of 1749 had increased the coaching trade through Ripley, adding much to the village's prosperity. Fresh horses could be hired for 1d a mile! This gradually died away when the railway to Portsmouth was completed in 1847. The poet and diarist A. J. Mumby, visiting Ripley in 1863, described the Talbot Inn as *a fine old coaching inn of forty years ago*, but by then the owner, John Metcalfe, employed only one ostler. Many years later, Harry's daughter Florence would become cook at the Talbot, and would say, "It was far enough away from London for them to misbehave, but close enough for them to be able to do so."

However, the National School continued to educate the village children and was funded by the church, local subscriptions, and a government grant. It was designed by Henry Woodyer, the Guildford architect, at a cost of £420. It seems an unlikely task for a man who is remembered for his churches and was influenced by Augustus Pugin. Woodyer was more a gentleman than a professional person. He was educated at Eton and Oxbridge, a son of a leading Guildford surgeon and the former Miss Mary Anne Eleanor Halsey of Henley Park, Normandy. It was also strange for such a man to design the House of Mercy (for fallen women) at Clewer, Windsor – a project close to the hearts of the politician William Gladstone and his wife. They hoped to help prostitutes reform their ways and lead more socially acceptable lives.

The 1851 census showed the population of southwest Surrey dramatically increasing. Improved transport links to the capital made the county more attractive to commuters, and the poor land which was unsuitable for farming began to interest developers. A school in Send was needed, and one was opened in October 1854. The architect was Mr Henry Peak. By 1859, an additional classroom was also needed for the Ripley school.

After 1854, the village school was renamed the Ripley National School, and a separate infant school was opened in 1861, in Rose Lane. This was built on a gift of land from Mrs Charles Marshall of Ripley Court, using money donated by her. It was known as Mrs Marshall's Infant School. The National School did not fund it, but nevertheless, Mrs Marshall received rent from the school managers. When the children *"came into an age of intelligence"*, they were transferred to the National School.

The reference to "national" shows the school was affiliated to the National Society for Promoting Education of the Poor in the Principles of the Church of England. It was one of the two societies allocated to administering the first grants of money to be given by the state towards the building of schools for the poor. The other society was the British and Foreign Schools Society. They had been doing so since 1813, working together with the Nonconformists.

The original aim of the Send and Ripley School was to educate eighty boys and eighty girls. They sat in one large hall. A moveable wooden screen divided it into two schoolrooms with separate entrances. Cut in stone above each one were the words "BOYS" and "GIRLS". Diocesan inspectors called regularly to make sure the children knew their catechism and Bible. The children were taught to arrange their letters and numbers using a sand tray. When they had reached perfection in these tasks, they then moved on to the next stage, using a slate and slate pencil. Each child was instructed to bring a rag from home to clean the slate.

Fixed to the walls were reading sheets. A child could not go up a stage until they could read every word correctly. It was the same with sums. After these tasks were completed, the children would turn to primers, a basic textbook. Cheap supplies of stationery, textbooks, and other educational materials were provided by the National Society.

The National Society did not motivate through the use of the cane, but by encouragement. The lady visitors often gave small prizes. One young girl, whose family moved to Ripley, proudly kept a copy of *Sunday Evenings: A book for girls who care to spend a few minutes each Sunday evening in quiet, thoughtful reading. A prize awarded by the EDUCATION BOARD of the Archdeaconry of Brecon: Examination in Religious Knowledge 1895. PRIZE awarded to Kate Mann: Scholar of the first division: Brecon National School.* Apart from daily religious education, the children were expected to attend church services and Sunday school. This often took place in the day school.

In 1862, a system of inspection was inaugurated. It was called inspection by results. Children were examined annually by Her Majesty's Inspectors (HMIs). The school received grants per head *only* if the inspectors were satisfied that each child had reached the required standards in reading, writing, and arithmetic. The grants were regulated by a child's record of attendance, which could be erratic.

If mother fell ill, a girl would be expected to stay at home to look after the younger children, or if the harvest was heavy, a boy would help out rather than waste time at school – and, of course, children were kept at home when the gypsies moved on. It was a known fact that they would steal a village child and force it into a life of slavery.

Many children had a long walk to school early in the morning, after first collecting milk from the farm. In the strawberry season, many children were sleepy because they had been out in the fields since 4 a.m. In fact, holidays were fixed during July and September to suit the needs of the country areas. The actual dates depended on the state of the crop.

When the children did manage to arrive at school, it would be early in the morning. On their arrival, they would often be grubby and dirty. Many of them had travelled across fields and along muddy lanes. Therefore, before lessons began, teacher inspected hands and fingernails for cleanliness. "Hair must be tied back and be clean, tidy and free from lice." Often, a little girl was embarrassed because the pinafore she wore over her dress was mucky and the *broderie anglaise* trimming torn and far from spotless.

Exercises during the morning helped to keep the children physically fit. This was known as drill. They marched military-style around the playground. At midday, the school closed for two hours. Those who lived nearby went home for their meal, but others who had a long walk ate their food at their desks.

Like many of her contemporaries, Harry's mother had little experience of school life. She could neither read nor write.

However, some children began to have a basic knowledge of sums and reading. Sadly, the Inspectorate was set up to make sure that the country received value for its money, thus only examinable subjects were taught – the result being that many people felt they never reached their full potential and later led frustrating lives.

However, the 1st Earl of Lovelace understood a young person's needs. His mother-in-law, Lady Byron, advocated the full development of the individual. She established a school in West London, Ealing Grove, which included practical tuition in allotment schemes, carpentry, masonry, and the commercial principles of marketing garden produce.

Lovelace was impressed, and set up a similar school in Ockham. Besides providing the normal school curriculum, there was a well-stocked library, three-and-a-half acres set aside for agricultural work, a small workshop for carpentry, basket making, a printing press, and gymnasium. Lessons were also given on the theory of music and natural philosophy. The principal aim of the school was to develop honest self-control.

It was not just education, but also the coming of the railways that widened horizons for ordinary people. There was no rail station at Ripley, and it remained something of a backwater. In 1851, many local folk boarded a train at Guildford or Woking Common to visit "The Great Exhibition of the Works of Industry of all Nations." Harry and his family did not go, but called to see their friend, Mr Chitty of Mill Street, Guildford, who displayed his flooring in the South Gallery of Crystal Palace and boasted to them, "They gave me a medal!"

Only thirteen years before, on 21st May 1838, a train ran for the first time from Nine Elms to Woking Common Station along the London to Southampton line. This was situated in bleak, gorse-filled heathland. In 1840, a railway hotel appeared, built next to the station. It possessed no stable accommodation.

Even twenty years later, only two buildings could be found within a half-mile radius of the station. However, at a meeting of the Railway Board in August 1838, it was reported that each week the average number of passengers was around 7,586, making a working profit of £8,770.

Woking Common found itself acting as the railhead for Guildford, Godalming, and much of rural Surrey as there was no other station between Weybridge and Farnborough. The main road to Portsmouth was nearby, and the stagecoaches which operated along the route were diverted to connect with the trains coming from and to London at Woking Common. The result was serious congestion. As the roads were narrow and often messy, coaches could hardly pass each other. Many Guildford inhabitants found it easier to go in their carriage to Woking Common, board the train at that station, and travel to London.

However, there were a few signs that indicated the railway network was going to be important. On 21st May 1838, Ditton Marsh station opened (it would later be rechristened Esher, serving Sandown Racecourse and Claremont House). Walton-on-Thames and Weybridge stations also opened between Nine Elms and Woking Common stations.

Harry did not travelled by rail until the 1870s. Hannah never did. Like Queen Victoria, many of her subjects were nervous of the speed of the train and feared a disaster, but for some businessmen, the coming of the railways spelt a serious financial loss.

On 10th October 1849, an advertisement in *The Times* announced an auction in the City of London: *FOURTEEN superior, good-sized seasoned horses, with their harness, the genuine property of Mr James Hay, which have been working a pair-horse carriage from Dorking to London and are to be sold in consequence of the opening of the Reading, Guildford and Reigate Railway.*

For many, the changes meant a better quality of life. Not only London could be reached quickly, but also the rest of the country. Wealthy men, tycoons, and professional men came to live close to Surrey's railway stations. Numerous horse-drawn coaches, carriages, and flies struggled along the muddy lanes, hoping to reach a station in time to catch the "London train".

However, these people brought the need for employment with them. They needed servants. Often, their houses were built at least five miles from the station and appeared at the end of long, curving drives, surrounded by several acres of garden, hidden behind shrubs, conifers, and banks of rhododendrons which thrived in Surrey's sandy soil. Occasionally, tennis courts, lawns, and swimming pools could be spied through the surrounding outbuildings. These housed servants, gardeners, stable lads, horses, and carriages. To some extent, this was a world on its own as neighbours could not easily be visited. They were usually at least a carriage-drive away.

At first, residential travel in Surrey was almost confined to the "gentry" and wealthier sections of the middle classes. In fact, many did not need to travel daily to work as they possessed private means. Even Queen Victoria, who rushed so fast to Claremont from Windsor that she left her equerry trailing behind her, splattered with mud, began to travel from Claremont along the London and Southampton railway. In 1837, the new Queen had come across construction works where a steam engine was hauling trucks over a contractor's track. She declared, "A curious thing indeed."

But for villages such as Ripley, which remained a distance from a railway station, life remained cut off. They found that coaches were travelling less along the Portsmouth Road. Eventually the stage ceased altogether, and sailors caught the train to Portsmouth. In 1869, a Kingston solicitor, Mr Bell, suggested a 3-foot-gauge rail line should run from the centre of Cobham to Esher station. This was thrown out. The more comfortable members of the village's 2,133 inhabitants continued to make do with the shilling Ripley-to-Esher horse bus. Presumably, Harry and his family walked or cadged a lift.

Nevertheless, there would be advantages. In August 1847, the *London Illustrated News* said, in their opinion, *"The Railways would benefit the Tourist Trade.*" People had more money to spare, and the railways brought Londoners cheaply, quickly, and relatively effortlessly into the Surrey countryside. Epsom rail station opened in 1847. William Powell Frith's *Derby Day* shows numerous thousands enjoying the race. In 1838, the Derby was moved to a Wednesday to fit in with the railway's timetable. The racecourse is not only famous for its great race, but also the appointment, in 1840, of Henry Dorling as Clerk to the Course. He was Mrs Beeton's stepfather.

When the owner of the haunted Hautboy (an old name for an oboe) & Fiddle Inn went bankrupt, Lord Lovelace replaced it, in 1864, with the much grander Hautboy Hotel. It was seen as an investment in the growing tourist trade. According to Mr Bashall, an expert supervising the process, the bending of the roof beams used steam heat.

The railways did not only bring tourism into Surrey, but also changed the pattern of work. Employment prospects continued to improve for domestic staff as more were required. To maintain status, a middle-class household must employ at least one servant. However, fewer men would be needed when the trains started to carry fuels, raw materials, chalk, stone, gravel, and Fuller's earth. They were cheaper and quicker than the lumbering horse-drawn vehicles struggling along soft-topped lanes. Surrey was not considered good agricultural country, but larger stocks of seeds, nitrogen fertilisers (guano), chemicals (mostly in powder form), and animal feed could now be brought to the farmers. Even the climate was slowly becoming warmer and helped to improve Surrey's agriculture.

The old woollen industry, which had been responsible for southwest Surrey's prosperity, had been in decline for many years. Fewer sheep appeared on the fields. The changes in the 19th century offered ordinary people opportunities to "better themselves", and self-help books abounded. By 1850, the country's population had increased to twenty-one million, but between 1815 and 1914, fifteen million people left England to improve their lives abroad. Many emigrated to the colonies and the New World.

The brighter, more adventurous farmers took to the new steam tractor. Here and there, a lone horseless tractor could be spotted. However, Surrey farmers still preferred to use horses to plough the county's tricky soil, and oxen had been used for centuries. In 1863, a visitor noticed a pair of Devonshire oxen ploughing a field near Wisley Heath. By this time, it had become an unusual sight. They were slow, ponderous animals, needing to stop for food often to rest and chew the cud.

As an agricultural labourer, Harry would have been affected by the growing middle-class demand for milk and meat products, so more cows appeared in the enlarged fields. Grass was replaced by root crops to feed the cattle, and fields enlarged to accommodate the larger agricultural machinery. In 1861, Mrs Beeton's *Book of Household Management* appeared, destined for the middle-class housewife who wished to eat salads and vegetables. Indeed, the whole world was changing, and the growth of the independent female was slowly emerging.

Harry and Hannah's daughter Ada would have envied Miss Jekyll's lifestyle. Her sister-in-law Agnes described her as *a pioneer spirit*. In later life, she would support the suffragette movement, but Gertrude Jekyll's life of independence only began when she was nearly eighteen. In 1861, with the support of her mother, she left Bramley to study at the Kensington School of Art. For the next two years, she travelled from Guildford station to London to attend classes in art and applied and decorative art, drawing being her major subject.

This happened in the year of the Prince Consort's death, and Queen Victoria found herself "a poor suffering creature". The Prince, not known for his liking for women's self-expression, had recommended a separate wing for female art students. Life classes were included, draped strategically for modestly. One young lady requested that "those of the male figures so shocking to behold should be covered".

Only one head teacher, male, took charge of the whole complex. Richard Burchett (1815–75) was a British artist of some renown. While at the school, Miss Jekyll made lifelong friendships with two other pupils: the sculptor Princess Louise, Queen Victoria's daughter, and the artist Helen Allingham, who painted delightful Surrey cottages utterly unlike the four-room cottage Harry and his family actually lived in.

During this time living in London, Miss Jekyll's horizons greatly expanded. Among the people she met was Gerald Grosvenor, Marquis of Westminster, later to be made the 1st Duke. Most importantly, Miss Jekyll became close to her father's friends Mr and Mrs Charles Newton. He was the Keeper of Antiquaries at the British Museum, and they were friendly with a friend of the Rev'd Dodgson – Alice Liddell of *Alice in Wonderland* fame. A tightly-knit group, London society weaved in and out, dancing around each other.

In 1863, the Newtons invited Miss Jekyll to travel with them to the Near East. Harry never travelled, and would have been amazed at 21st-century package holidays. The Newtons and Miss Jekyll probably crossed the English Channel in a sailing boat; although steam was available, few used it. After coping with dangerous roads, brigands, and small earthquakes, the party returned to England on Boxing Day. The day after they disembarked, their ship was wrecked. Gertrude Jekyll returned to Bramley and continued her life.

By 1861, the nineteen-year-old Harry had already been working for nearly ten years. The census lists him as an agricultural labourer living with his parents. He may have already been working for a tenant of Lord Lovelace's, Arthur Lambert of Bridgefoot Farm. He was a man William Cobbett would have described as being of *plain manners and plentiful living*.

The farm lies on the corner of the Portsmouth Road as winds its way towards London, opposite the wrought-iron gates of Ockham Park. Once, the estate belonged to the Westons. Lord Byron's only legitimate daughter, Ada, called it home. It was purchased by Lord King in 1711, and redesigned in 1729–30, to designs by Nicholas Hawksmoor.

However, no architect altered Bridgefoot Farm. It grew "topsy-like" during the 18th and 19th centuries, but in the brick-work is carved "1624", hinting at an earlier existence. The house would have contained two areas: one for service, where brewing, laundering, and dairying would have taken place; the other for living. At the rear is an extension, the kitchen, built of larger brick. It contained a bread oven, bacon oven, boiling copper, and a great fireplace. Settles were placed on either side, with Windsor chairs scattered around and burnished copper pans sitting on shelves around the room. In the centre of the kitchen stood a sturdy wooden table, large enough for the whole house-hold to sit round. Mr Lambert employed twenty-five agricultural labourers.

His wife Anne had died in about 1846. She had produced eight children in thirteen years. The household was run by his sister-in-law, Frances Eagren, known as Fanny, and Mary, his daughter. They were responsible for making butter, cheese, clotted cream, and smoking and curing meats with the help of a maid-of-all-work, Emma Billinghurst. A male farm servant assisted with the heavier work. There were two boys around the place, Thomas and William Lee, who may have been related to Arthur Lambert. It often happened that parents farmed out chil-dren to wealthier relatives. The kitchen is where Harry would have eaten, done business with "master", and felt at home. It was the focus of the house for everybody, where they all met, sooner or later. Harry would never have entered the parlour. That was only used on high days, holidays, and funerals.

Thirty metres distant from the house still stands an impres-sive barn. At some stage "wain" (wagon) doors were inserted, giving access to a threshing floor which is said to have been made of stones from Newark Abbey. In the grounds to the north of the house is a "ha-ha", constructed to prevent farm animals straying from the fields into the formal gardens. It is known that

Arthur Lambert kept a carter and a cow man. Later, Harry gives himself as stockman at Bridgefoot Farm.

Harry may have seen a dreamy young man, Arthur Mumby, who walked around *the thriving village of Ripley* while staying with a friend. One Saturday in May 1863, the civil servant, together with his friend Alfred Lane, Royal Academy artist, caught the 2:20 p.m. train from Waterloo station and arrived at Weybridge station at 3:30 p.m.

The two men walked through Weybridge Common, *brilliant with gorse and broom; after a mile or so of road beyond it, we crossed the little river Wey . . . passing several 17th and 18th century houses of good size. In the arable fields men were hoeing here and there and once or twice woman, alone.* When the couple arrived in Ripley, Mumby found that Lane lived in a labourer's cottage. It contained a sitting room, scullery, and pantry, and a quaint stair wound up into two little bedrooms. It cost Lane half a crown a week. A woman of the village came in at times, and acted as his servant.

This may have also been the girl who looked after Mumby. He described her in his diary: *Esther is a girl of two and twenty or so, a great pet (artistically speaking) of Lane's and mine.* She was probably Esther Whitbourne, whose family farmed 104 acres at West Horsley.

Mumby wrote in his diary of 4th March 1863, *Lane tells me that the Surrey folks of Ripley are more primitive than many in far off countries. They keep up the old merriment and village customs. They still play football in the streets on Shrove Tuesday and turn out on Guy Fawkes Day for a long procession of masks and mummers. They still pursue every cruel husband with the Nemesis of marrowbones and cleavers. But then they are six miles from a railway and have no other channel of intercourse with London, than a weekly carrier's cart.*

Mumby was obviously unaware that several of the village men were employed by the Soda Water Company. However, Harry seems to have been more sophisticated than many of his contemporaries, perhaps influenced by regular contact with the

great and the good. Harry, who could read and write, helped his
father with the duties of sexton at the parish church.

The entries in the church accounts continue:

July 1864, Paid Worsfold from Stoke: 2 days work
             Repairing church gate 5/-
             Clipping hedge 2/-

Christmas 1864: G Worsfold 10/-

July 1867, Paid Worsfold's bill until Christmas, £4 2s 7d
July 1869 Paid Worsfold (sexton) repairing vestry chair 3/-

For church funds: In the New Year of 1868:

Earl of Onslow donated £3 4 4d.
Earl of Lovelace donated 7/-

Arthur Mumby, as did most of the villagers, appreciated
Ripley's Green. He described it *as free to all and always*. The agricultural writer Arthur Young said *the poor are injured by the
Enclosure Acts. They are deprived many of an important means of
support. The poor could feed their cows and geese on common land and
most importantly it was a source of free fuel*. Although 600 acres of
land in the parish had been enclosed under the Enclosure Act of
1803, Ripley Green remained common land and cricket
continued to be played on it. Harry never played cricket. He said
he had not the time for sports, but he boasted that "Lumpy
Stevens" played on Ripley Green, and recited the verse *For honest
Lumpy did allow. He ne'er would pitch o'er a brow*. Short, round-
shouldered, and stout, he seemed an unlikely candidate to be
given the accolade *the greatest bowler ever*.

A professional cricketer, Lumpy was born at Send in 1735.
In 1775, he played a famous game in Portsmouth. This was
between five of the Hambledon Club and five of the All-
England Club. He threw the ball, bowling three times, between
the two stumps of John Smith, Hambledon's last man, and

bowled him out. Smith complained. Subsequently, three wickets were introduced.

A gardener, Lumpy worked for his sponsor, Lord Tankerville of Walton-on-Thames, who was responsible for drawing up the rules of cricket, including "leg before wicket". Lumpy also won a £100 bet for Lord Tankerville. He hit a feather within four balls. Lumpy died in 1819, at eighty-four years of age. He lies buried in St Mary's churchyard, Walton-on-Thames.

While Lord Tankerville enjoyed cricket, the widowed 3rd Earl of Onslow, Arthur George, remained a recluse in Richmond. Harry and Hannah were sympathetic. They knew of the donations His Lordship gave to Ripley parish church. The lives of country people were entwined with those of the gentry even though theirs were more interesting and dramatic. However, their good or bad fortune affected "the lower orders", most of whom depended upon them directly or indirectly. In 1856, the 3rd Earl had received a second, devastating blow. At only thirty-six years of age, Viscount Cranley, his only son, died. This left no direct heir to inherit Clandon. By 1841, the "great house" possessed a forlorn and deserted air; repairs fell into abeyance, most of the pictures and furniture had been removed. In fact, the estate reflected His Lordship's depression.

In 1830, Onslow had received his first shock when his beloved Countess died. Immediately he ordered her apartments to be closed, leaving them just as she had left them. Even the piece of work on which she was working remained with the needle sticking out of its reel of cotton. By 1841, the census reported that Mrs Dallen, the housekeeper, and a young female companion lived in the house, lighting fires and opening windows. Edmund Hook, gamekeeper, also lived at Clandon. He provided security and helped with the heavy duties. And so life continued in "Miss Haversham" style until the arrival of the young 4th Earl in 1870.

In 1857, an eccentric, non-cricket-playing man inherited Sutton Place. He was Francis Henry Salvin of Croxdale Hall,

County Durham, and was the residuary legatee of the will of Captain John Joseph Webbe-Weston. Through his mother's side, Salvin was related to an ancient family known throughout Yorkshire and County Durham. As a Roman Catholic, Salvin remained a recusant, unable to take any part in public life. He was seen by the locals as a foreigner and a subject of interest.

The property did not come with free possession. In 1855, it was tenanted by Charles LeFevre. This was followed by another tenant, Caledon Alexander. Salvin never married. Unlike the 3rd Earl of Onslow, he did not live as a recluse, but modestly in Woking. He enjoyed practical jokes, field sports, fishing for cormorants, and keeping otters, training one to follow him and sleep on his lap. His pet pig was called "Lady Susan". He placed a collar and lead on a prize boar and took it for walks. Salvin was a much-respected expert on falconry and wrote a book on the subject in 1855, with William Brodrick: Falconry in the British Isles. A first edition was auctioned at Bonhams, in June 2012, for £2,500.

In 1874, Salvin leased Sutton Place to Frederick Harrison. It remained with that family until 1900, when the newspaper magnate Lord Northcliffe leased the estate.

Harry held in the highest esteem William King, 1st Earl of Lovelace. He was a Whig, like his father Peter King, 7th Baron King of Ocham, and admired for his qualities as a landowner and his considerable intellect. As a young man, the 1st Earl of Lovelace entered the diplomatic service. He could speak French, Italian, Spanish, and Modern Greek fluently. He travelled throughout Arabia and Egypt, and had conversations with Muhammad Ali Pasha, the father of modern Egypt, who reigned from 1805 until 1848, organised Egyptian society, streamlined the economy, established a professional bureaucracy, and built up the modern army. The dynasty of Muhammad Ali Pasha lasted until 1952.

In 1839, the young Lovelace had undertaken, "not without the utmost diffidence, on the morning of the loyal address, in answer from the throne, on the opening of the new Parliamentary session to the Queen's speech". In 1840, he became Lord Lieutenant of Surrey and the leading figure in the county. A year later, Lord Lovelace was elected a fellow of the Royal Society of Arts.

In 1852, his wife Ada, Countess of Lovelace, died aged thirty-six – the same age as her father, Lord Byron, had. She was his only legitimate child. When she married the Earl in 1835, Ada brought with her £30,000 in cash, vast estates in the Midlands, and the "eye and ear" of her cousin, Whig Prime Minister Lord Melbourne, the Queen's favourite, together with the goodwill of his wife, the former Lady Caroline Lamb. She is remembered for becoming unhinged by her passion for Lord Byron and shattered by the remarks of her promiscuous husband: "You are prudish and strait-laced." Ada produced three children: Byron, styled Viscount Ockham, later 12th Baron Wentworth (1836–62), Lady Annabella, later 1st Baroness Wentworth (1837–1917), and Ralph Gordon, styled Viscount Ockham, later 2nd Earl of Lovelace (1839–1906).

A few months before her death, Ada confessed a secret to her husband. Immediately he abandoned her. A brilliant mathematician, she was the first computer programmer, called by her colleague Charles Babbage *the enchantress of Numbers*. Ada became addicted to prescription drugs such as opium and morphine, dying deeply in debt. It was rumoured she had had an affair with a fellow gambler. Harry would not have known that the work of Ada Lovelace would help transform the lives of his great-grandchildren, and a computer language, used by the United States Department of Defence, would be called Ada in her memory.

After his wife's death, the Earl travelled extensively. Onboard ship, he met Mrs Jane Jenkins Crawford, the widow of a Bengal civil servant, daughter of a Calcutta auctioneer. She had three sons. In 1865, the couple married. As Lady Lovelace, Jane produced one child, Lionel Fortescue King Noel. He became the 3rd Earl and the last earl of Lovelace to live in Surrey.

Mrs Jenkins had married Surrey's greatest landowner. Since becoming the 1st Earl, Lovelace had bought lands in Pyford, Wisley, and East Clandon. In 1860, Ada's mother, Anne Isabella Noel Byron, 11th Baroness Wentworth, died of breast cancer. She left her vast estates to her son-in-law on one condition – that he added Noel to his surname.

By being an improving landlord, Lovelace continued to increase the value of his estates. In 1860, he embarked in East Surrey on an extensive building programme. He even turned his attention to East Horsley's butcher, village shop, and Wellington Inn, which had enjoyed several names, including The Greyhound and The Crown, following the restoration of the monarchy in 1660.

The inn was built facing the village street, but when Charles Barry rebuilt it, under instructions from a predecessor of Lord Lovelace's, in 1758, it was turned around to face the new Turnpike Road, which was seeing an increase in traffic. The inn was renamed the Duke of Wellington after the "Iron Duke". It remained a coaching inn.

A coach left early every morning for the Spur Inn, Borough High Street, London, and returned every evening. Twice a week, a wagon went up to London via Epsom, and there was a daily service to Guildford. When Leatherhead station opened in 1868, a wagonette called there every morning and evening. A small single-story room served as the ticket office for people wishing to use the coach. The "Duke" had three guest rooms and stabling for six horses. In the yard, a couple of cottages housed two coachmen and an ostler, together with three pigsties.

No Surrey landlord, other than Lord Lovelace, could have made it clearer that this part of the county was his personal domain, with its buildings of brick and flint facings, metal windows, and embellishing friezes of terracotta tiles. Lord Lovelace may have been an amateur, self-taught engineer, but in 1849, he addressed the Institute of Civil Engineers, so impressing the members – even Isambard Kingdom Brunel – that the Society invited him to become a member.

Sometime after 1855, Lovelace put his architectural and engineering mind to rebuilding his main home, East Horsley Place. He was determined to give his Surrey estate the Gothic facelift worthy of the county's most important inhabitant. Lovelace transformed the whole so much so that Mathew Arnold described Horsley Towers as *fantastic*, and Ian Nairn and Nicholas Pevsner exclaimed *the main drive must be one of the most sensational in England*. Lovelace even designed bridges in a horse-shoe style to go over gullies, allowing him to cut through the surrounding woods. The 1st Earl of Lovelace was justifiably proud of his achievements, and Harry, working and living on his lands, was proud of such a gentleman.

Lord Lovelace may have enjoyed being successful, but his eldest son, Byron Noel Viscount Ockham, later known as Baron Wentworth, was unsuited to his position in life. He joined the Royal Navy, and deserted ship en route to the Crimea. Subsequently, he put aside his title and became known to his fellow navvies as "Ockham", working as a manual labourer on the Isle of Dogs. Harriet Beecher Stowe met him at a social function in the 1850s, which she was attending with his grandmother, Lady Byron. The author was struck *by a wonderful development of physical and muscular strength*. Lady Byron agreed, saying *he has a body that required more vigorous animal life than his station gives him scope for*. At the time of the meeting with Harriet Stowe, Baron Wentworth was engaged on the ironwork of the Great Eastern. Lady Byron hoped that *Ockham is now going through an experience which may yet fit him to do great good when he comes to the peerage*.

It did not. On 1st September 1862, he died of a burst blood vessel. He was twenty-six years old. Subsequently, Lady Byron took over the upbringing of Ralph, Lovelace's second son, creating him the 13th Baron Wentworth.

Ada's daughter Annabella, 15th Baroness Wentworth, married, on 8 June 1869, Wilfred Scawen Blunt, famed for his erotic poetry. She became known as Lady Anne Blunt and had inherited something of her father's brilliance. Lady Anne spoke French, German, Italian, Spanish, and Arabic fluently. She played the violin superbly, and studied drawing under John Ruskin. Like most members of the English aristocracy, she loved horses as much as Blunt loved women. His marriage did not stop him having numerous affairs, often with more than one woman at a time. Lady Anne continually mourned her many miscarriages. However, the couple did have one child, Judith, born on 6th February 1873. In the late 1870s, they travelled to Cairo and the Middle East, buying Arabian horses from Bedouin tribesmen. The Blunts founded the Crabbet Arabian Stud. Most good racehorses are descended from this stud.

Eventually, Lady Anne and Wilfred Scawen Blunt parted. She spent her last days living in Egypt, often wearing Bedouin dress. Judith suffered from an unhappy marriage as well, but enjoyed breeding horses and King Charles' spaniels.

Meanwhile, the More-Molyneuxs of Loseley Park were having problems. Aunt Jane had died, and Colonel Thomas's son George inherited Loseley. In 1820, he demolished the west wing, together with the indoor riding school. George justified his actions as "the house was badly maintained and there was no money to restore it." He sold some of the pictures in the gallery and moved others into the main house. The loss of the staff bedrooms upset the servants. New, tiny staff bedrooms "mushroomed" in the Long Gallery. The family chapel was closed.

In 1876, the third church of St Nicholas was built in Bury Fields, Guildford, and contains the Loseley Chapel where generations of More-Molyneux lie buried. This is all that remains of the original medieval church. Despite all that George did, the old Mulberry tree continues to grow in the park – legend has it that when it is blown down, the More-Molyneuxs will die out.

Guildford remained Harry's market town. Animals were sold at the bottom of the High Street until 1865, when the market moved into North Street. Harry, as a stockman, always did business over a pint in the farmers' inn, the Bull's Head, opposite Tunsgate. Throughout the 19th century, heavy drinking remained a problem throughout Surrey. In 1865, a local man, Thomas Taunton, bought a flour mill at the bottom of the town and built a brewery on the land, using hops grown around Farnham and as far away as Petersfield, Hampshire. Throughout the 19th century, heavy drinking remained one of Surrey's most serious problems.

The brewery became one of Guildford's largest employers, and the smell of malted barley filled Harry's nostrils as he walked around the town. He probably never gave a thought to the Black Friars who had once wandered around the town preaching and praying.

By the 1890s, the population had increased to 9,000. In 1864, the Borough Council had appointed its first surveyor, Mr Henry Peak. On 2nd April 1864, a monthly sheet appeared, the *Surrey & Hants Advertiser and Commercial and Agricultural Register*. This communicated directly with the inhabitants and had a guaranteed circulation of 3,000 copies. It was the brainchild of Joseph Whittaker Barfott who, among other things, was Secretary of the West Surrey Permanent Mutual Benefit Building Society.

On 30th April, the sheet informed its readers that *it would appear on the first Saturday of every month, would be circulated free, among all classes of the community, and sent to inns, public institutions, coffee-rooms and upwards of five hotels, in Surrey, Hants, Sussex and Middlesex.*

On 2nd July 1864, the newspaper announced *today we combine local news and local articles with our advertisement sheet. This we have done in accordance with a promise made in our pages two months ago. We have also to announce in future the Surrey Advertiser will be published twice a month – the first Saturday in the month and the third*

Saturday in the month. Among the numerous advertisements on the front page, these appeared:

Mr Henry Peak: Drawings, Specifications and Estimates.

George Head Wine, Spirit and Bottled Ale Merchant: Bass's Bottled Ale - Pints 3s 6d Quarts 6s 6d per dozen

George Hawkins, Silversmith, Jeweller and Watchmaker Pawnbroker, and General Outfitter

By 30th July 1864, the strategy had been changed. The *Surrey Advertiser* was being sold weekly at 1d a copy. A year later, Mr T. D. Lysaght was appointed editor. In October 1865, the *Surrey Advertiser* was being produced by the company's own staff, and Harry and Hannah were among its readers.

In 1868, Guildford High Street was paved with setts, and described by Charles Dickens as "the most beautiful street in England". It may have been, but Surrey faced an agricultural depression which would last for the next thirty years.

CHAPTER THREE

The 1870s

Depression, Lily Wilson and the Last of the Parish Constables

The "Hungry Forties" were over, the fifties and sixties had gone, and now the 1870s approached, bringing with them poor harvests and depression. This spread throughout the countryside and would last for nearly thirty years. It all began in 1873, when the USA plunged Europe into the "Long Depression" because the world price of grain fell, together with the prices of other agricultural produce. Britain's "policy of free trade" exacerbated the situation. Cheap food in the form of grains flooded into the country from the USA, together with other agricultural products. During this time, Harry had a wife and family to clothe and feed.

Due to the advent of new machinery and changes in agricultural practices, farmers did not need so many workers. A transient workforce was more useful to them. Country people like Harry understood the land, but the new type of labourers did not. They neither knew nor cared. A continual series of bad harvests and imports from the prairies dramatically lowered the prices which the farmers would receive, and affected Harry's wages.

The 1871 census shows Harry, at thirty years of age, and Hannah, two years his senior, with growing responsibilities. They were bringing up three children in a four-room cottage with an outside privy. The family consisted of Montague, 5 years old, Martha, 3, and Ada-Jane, just a month, together with Alice Daws, four. She is reported as a boarder and does not appear in the Ripley school lists nor is ever mentioned again. In the next census, they would have two more children, Mary and Fanny, who are listed as pupils at Ripley National School.

Harry claimed to be the last surviving parish constable. He held this position for two years, but left when the Surrey County Constabulary became properly established. The Surrey Police Museum has no record of him holding this appointment, but he did say he lived in Ockham and for a time worked for Lord Lovelace. His son, Percy, was born in Ockham in 1875. The last parish constable of Ockham was appointed in 1872 (no name is given). As a sexton of Ripley parish church, Harry was a suitably respectable person.

He was proud that his appointment was made by the church-wardens and not by the ratepayers en bloc, which was the more usual. Harry received payment for his services, received a truncheon and a heavy grey greatcoat for winter nights. As a sign of office, he was presented with a tricorne hat. Harry's main concerns were the danger of fire, misbehaving youths, bawdy behaviour in inns, and drunken soldiers and sailors en route to and from Portsmouth. Lone "dollies" arrived with their gentlemen at the Talbot Inn. The gentlemen left early next morning – alone. The women often needed money to return to London. They plied their trade up and down Ripley High Street.

Violent crime such as murder or robbery was rare, but whatever happened, it was Harry who apprehended the miscreants and placed them in the village lockup. It was not his duty to prosecute, but that of the victim. However, he escorted the offenders to the magistrates' court in Guildford. There seemed to be some rivalry between the parish constables and the county police. Harry told the tale of the mystery of the disappearing strawberries: he advised a young constable to ask an older colleague to remove his helmet. The strawberries came cascading down.

An additional worry facing Harry was Lady Agnes. It was known she possessed a magnificent emerald brooch and earrings. Harry asked her, "Are they safe, my lady?"

She glared at him. "Mr Worsfold, they are kept here, close to my heart." She pointed to her bosom. "I assure you, no man will get his hands on them."

Harry had left school automatically at ten. He found his children did not. In order for them to do so, the authorities made certain demands: they must pass the Second Standard and have attended school at least 250 times over the previous two years.

All teachers at a village National School faced the same problems: the resentment of parents and constant absenteeism of the children. Ever since the Ripley school had opened, masters and mistresses came and went, except for Mr and Mrs Joseph Lewis. They were made of sterner stuff, and lasted for eleven years. However, changes were coming. England faced tough competition from the growth of world industrialisation. The country was no longer easily the workshop of the world, but younger, tougher competitors fought for the same markets. Businessmen feared the country's rivals and knew that, in order to combat them, it was necessary to have an intelligent, educated workforce.

For these reasons, on 17th February 1870, education changed forever. The Liberal member of Parliament, William Forster, introduced the Elementary Education Act, called by many "Forster's Education Act". It set the framework for children's education from five to thirteen years of age. Prime Minister Gladstone, so admired by Harry, was not keen. Like many a deeply religious person, his chief concern was for the child's soul. It was essential that they learnt the basic principles of the Christian faith.

Others remained hostile to the education of the masses. They feared they may start "to think" and become dissatisfied with their lot. The Act upset the Nonconformists because of the ways in which religion was to be taught. The Church authorities saw the Act as a threat to their hold on young minds. MP Forster was considered to be betraying both factions. He was born a Nonconformist and a Quaker. On his marriage to the daughter of Dr Thomas Arnold, headmaster of Rugby School, he had joined the Church of England and became a member of the establishment.

The Act did not make education compulsory or free, but it did establish a system of elective school boards. These filled the gaps in areas not covered by the voluntary bodies, either by building new schools or taking over inefficient ones. The school boards levied rates, provided teachers, and insisted that those children who were not receiving other forms of instruction attended school.

In Ripley, the Church was unhappy about the likely outcome of the Act. Fortunately, the report for the Ripley National School in 1871 was favourable. There was enough accommodation for the 156 children, plus eighty-three infants in Mrs Marshall's school. There was no need for the School Board to take control, much to the relief of the Master, Mr James W. Strictland, and his sister Harriet, the schoolmistress.

In 1876, attendance at school became compulsory. The following year, the first paid School Attendance Officer was appointed by the Board of Guardians in Guildford. This covered the parishes of Ripley, Send, Ockham, and Wisley. Mr Charles P. Frye's salary was £80 a year. His duties included visiting schools and checking registers, seeking out children of school age in his district, ensuring they attended school regularly, and reminding parents of the financial penalties incurred if they did not send their children to school. He then had to spend time searching high and low for those children who were absent, and make sure they were not out at work. Parents and employers tried to ignore the law, but Mr Frye carried out his tasks with such diligence that he gradually changed the situation.

In 1877, new government guidelines demanded that a certificate had to be issued by the School Attendance

Committee in Guildford. This was set up by the Board of Guardians. Before a child could leave school, new criteria were demanded: they must have reached a particular standard, attended school a certain number of times, and –most importantly – have suitable employment to go to.

For fourteen years Mr Frye served his parishes well, but in May 1890, the School Attendance Committee received a complaint: he had not visited Ripley school for six months. On his last visit, the Master had been forced to ask Mr Frye to leave for using bad language in front of the children. Sadly, a year later, he suffered a nervous breakdown. Mr Frye disappeared into the Surrey lunatic asylum and was heard of no more.

He would have found much to occupy him. The hospital possessed a dairy farm, cobbler's shop, and a large ballroom. In 1875, it had 672 patients; half were women. Patients who could do so worked in the various departments of the asylum, cleaning, washing, and carrying out repairs. Many women considered employment in the laundry the most desirable occupation. The asylum possessed its own gasworks, fire brigade, and sewerage works. It was the largest such establishment in West Surrey; built on Knaphill Common, close to Woking, it used the services of many local businesses and was itself a major employer in the area.

Meanwhile, a new employer was coming into the area – a great garden was being created at Wisley. The Royal Horticultural Society benefited from the business skills of a keen new member. One of thirteen children, George Fergusson Wilson was born in Wandsworth, in 1822. A bachelor, he came to live in Weybridge at Gishurst Cottage, next door to Bartropp's, where his sister lived. Their father had been a merchant in Russia, and on his return to England, founded a candle-making firm in Battersea, E. Price & Son. Wilson worked for his father, commuting daily.

On his return, he pruned his fruit trees by candlelight, working late into the evenings. In 1855, he built a greenhouse in his garden and began entering horticultural shows. Gardening turned into a passion when he won first prize with his pears. In a sale, he bought some sea-damaged lily bulbs and successfully grew them inside his greenhouse and in the garden. Wilson began collecting "all the known lilies of the world" and was awarded twenty Royal Horticultural Society (RHS) first-class certificates for his lilies, and became known as "Lily Wilson".

Perhaps some of his horticultural success was due to his training as a chemist. He researched and patented a process by which cheap, malodorous fats could be utilised in the place of tallow for candle making. The invention was profitable and, in 1847, the business was sold for £250,000. A new company, Price's Patent Candle Company, was formed with Wilson and his brother James as managing directors. He continued to improve and research new products for the company. In 1863, at the age of thirty-nine, he retired and resigned his managing directorship. The next year, he married Miss Ellen Barchard of Wandsworth. They produced two sons and a daughter.

The RHS had suffered mixed fortunes since its inception, in 1804, as the London Horticultural Society. Financially, it lurched from crisis to crisis. In 1818, it leased land in Kensington to create a garden, but by 1822, more land was needed as collectors were sending so many plants home. Subsequently, thirty-three acres were leased in Chiswick. By 1857, it had become an unfashionable area, and visitor numbers dropped. It was suggested that Chiswick should only be used for trial gardens. Soon the contents were sold and a small sum of money was raised. A couple of years later, 221 to 222 acres were leased in South Kensington with the aim of creating a plea-sure garden and a venue for shows.

The 1860s were a particularly turbulent time for the RHS. The patronage of the Prince Consort had been much valued, and his support had increased the number of fellows. Following Prince Albert's death, the Society changed its name to the Royal

Horticultural Society and faced up to its financial problems. It is not known when Wilson first became a fellow, but by 1865, it is recorded he had become a council member and was soon on several committees. Wilson was treasurer from 1866–68, and at various times he chaired the Floral Committee and the Fruit Committee. At one time he was Vice-President. By the 1870s, the lease on the Kensington garden was terminated.

At the same time, pollution was ruining Chiswick garden, and indifferent transport meant that the spring shows were poorly attended. From 1862, for twenty-six years, the site of the Great Spring Show was Kensington Gardens.

Wilson felt that if the Society was to survive, it must change. In 1874, he published a pamphlet, *The Royal Horticultural Society: As It is and as It Might Be*, suggesting that the two factions should have a garden each. The society could become solvent if the number of members was raised to 500 and they were charged a subscription of a guinea each. The new members should have an interest in horticulture and want to further its interests. Wilson's solutions were generally agreed to by the members. He is credited with saving the society by raising extra funds.

During the late 1870s, rents – even for the best land – had fallen to 8s to 12s an acre, and the great estates themselves were in difficulty. In 1878, Wilson learned that in the village of Wisley, Oakwood was for sale, cheaply. Four miles from Weybridge, the gardens lay on the Portsmouth Road between Cobham and Woking, surrounded by heathlands. Harry rarely wandered down Wisley Lane. It ran off the Portsmouth Road through "scattered farms and cottages".

Far down the lane, tucked away behind a barn, stands an ancient church. Its dedication remains a mystery, but the *advowson* (the right to grant the beneficiary) belonged to the powerful Onslows. The lane continues winding its way on for another mile or so until it reaches Pyrford Lock and the bridge over the River Wey.

Oakwood was just what Wilson needed. The highly acid, peculiar soil was ideal for him to create his "experimental" garden. It allowed him to grow rhododendrons, lilies, irises, and the thousands of other plants which collectors brought back with them from strange lands. Wilson carefully documented everything he did and wrote about his horticultural activities in numerous articles and journals.

Slowly, his fame spread – especially his success with lilies. Visitors flocked to Oakwood, including Miss Jekyll who, on return from her exile in Wargrave, exclaimed, "I have had the happiness of visiting Mr G. F. Wilson's garden at Wisley, a garden which I take to be about the most instructive it is possible to see!"

In 1868, Miss Jekyll had returned from Italy, its warmth, light, and culture making her see life through "new eyes". However, a change of circumstance meant she must leave Surrey, where she felt she belonged. Her father owned a property, Wargrave Hill in Berkshire. It was left to him by his father. While Miss Jekyll had been in Italy, its elderly tenant died and thus ended the long lease. On 8th June 1868, Miss Jekyll arrived in Berkshire. She loathed Wargrave *because it was not Surrey*. She kept in touch with Bramley, but found travelling to London more difficult. The Great Western Railway Company did not provide a station at Wargrave as Twyford was considered to be close enough. The train was slow, taking its time; eventually, Miss Jekyll arrived at Paddington.

In 1878, while Gertrude Jekyll was fighting her change of circumstances, the RHS faced yet another financial crisis: London smog and pollution forced the Council to consider moving its gardens outside London. It is thought that Wilson offered the Society Oakwood. If so, nothing came of it.

As the RHS struggled, the Onslows also faced a serious problem. In the autumn of 1870, the ninety-three-year-old 3rd Earl of Onslow died a bitter old man. His heir was a boy of seventeen, not even a close relative, and one he did not care for.

His only son, Viscount Cranley, had died at only thirty-six years of age.

Hillier Onslow was only two years old when his father died. The boy slowly learned that the great derelict mansion, *built for entertaining*, was to be his destiny. The family did not even invite Hillier to his great-uncle's funeral. However, others expected great things from the new 4th Earl. His classics master at Eton, Arthur James, described the young man as *pretty well the tallest, least embarrassed and most self possessed young man whom I had ever had the pleasure of meeting.*

On 2nd November 1870, when the old Earl had been dead for less than a week, "Hillie", as his family called him, came to Clandon. He wrote in his diary *the inside is in a very fair state of preservation considering it's not been touched for forty-three years though all the blinds, curtains, etc. had perished. The stories describing Clandon as in a near-derelict state are exaggerated: grass is not growing up through the slabs in the marble hall, nor is the window glass broken and nor is the place devoid of pictures and furniture.*

In fact, when Hillier entered the marble hall, he would have been made aware of the power of the Onslows: the walls stretch up to the attics; "Michelangelo" figures sprawl languorously across the ceiling; over the doorways, between broken pied-monts, two marble blackamoors peer down. They are a reminder to visitors that *this house was built by toiling under the Jamaican sun.* Sacrificial scenes are carved on the chimney breasts. The right-hand one bears the signature of Jan Michiel Rysbruck (John Michael Rysbruck) from Antwerp, the most famous sculptor of his day.

The hall is so large that, in 1874, the Earl could comfortably host a luncheon for 110 people. The principal guest was Henry Pelham, 6th Duke of Newcastle-under-Lyme. At the far end of the room was Francis Barlow's paintings of an ostrich and Cawsey watch, appearing to say to guests, "Here is a family of much erudition." Such exotic birds would be found only in the menageries of royalty or the very rich.

There were other things in Clandon Park to impress Hillier, such as the embroidery of the hangings and covers of the Tudor four-poster state bed. He may not have known his family had been Francophiles, and in 1791, the last person to sleep in it was the murdered Princess de Lamballe. She was a friend of Marie Antoinette and superintendent of the Queen's household.

On her return to France, the Princess was tried by a "kangaroo court", together with Madame de Tourzel, governess to the Royal children. The two women were thrown into the notorious La Force Prison, together with Pauline, Madame de Tourzel's daughter.

The highly-strung Princess was dragged out by the mob and hideously murdered (some say raped), mutilated, and even her breasts cut off. She was certainly decapitated. The Princess had been a gentle, loving woman known for her charitable works, but the young girl survived. On the evening of the executions, a mysterious stranger arrived and took Pauline away with him. The man was Monsignor Hardy, the real Scarlet Pimpernel.

When they were naughty, Hannah frightened her children with "Old Boney will get you!" Delaroche's painting of *Bonaparte crossing the Alps* caught Hillier's eye. The Emperor is seated upon an Alpine pony led by a plodding guide. He may have been surprised to learn that it was painted at the instigation of his great-uncle. In 1848, when the 3rd Earl visited the Louvre, he found David's painting implausible and over-theatrical. He commissioned Delaroche to paint a historically accurate picture, which is now in the Walker Gallery, Liverpool, and another version in the Louvre. This Napoleon is a subdued and thoughtful figure. His cloak is fastened tight against the snow and ice. The 3rd Earl did not entirely waste his life. He collected Old Masters, Sevres china, French furniture, and portrait busts.

Hillier soon moved into Clandon Park. He made his apartments in Lady Henrietta's bedroom, dressing room, and library. The spirit of the 1st Earl's wife did not complain. However, the ghost of Elizabeth Knight, the wife of the 2nd Lord Onslow, dressed in a white ballgown, wanders from room to room clutching a hunting knife. It is said she is inspecting the house built with her inheritance, and which she never saw, dying of smallpox before it was completed. Speaker Onslow described Lady Elizabeth as "a woman of the truest goodness of mind and heart I have ever known". Why such a gentle creature roams around Clandon clutching a dangerous knife, dagger-like, has never been explained.

Hillier was able to start planning improvements due to the growth of Guildford's prosperity and selling land to the railway company. He had the house redecorated, probably using his mother Mary Loftus' knowledge of drapery. He modernized Clandon, central heating was installed, the house connected to the mains water, and proper drains dug. The young Earl improved his tenants' cottages and farms which had remained untouched for years. In fact, he became much loved and known as "Hillier" to everybody.

His tenants and friends were delighted when, on 3rd February 1875, the Earl married the Hon. Florence Coulson Gardener at St George's Church, Hanover Square. She was the daughter of Alan Legge, 3rd Lord Gardener, and his second wife, Drury Lane actress Julia Sarah Hayfield Fortescue. Polite society never accepted her as she had been her husband's mistress. Their eldest son, Herbert, was born prior to his parents' marriage. He was a love child and thus unacceptable as his father's heir.

After his marriage, Hillier began to take a more active part in local and national affairs. He continued to be interested in hunting and shooting. A gifted amateur actor, he took part in a now unknown play, *Chiselling*. The performance was given in a "spacious noble room", the principal drawing room, the Palladio Room. "Les Deux Pigeons" observed the proceedings from their place on the Reveillon wallpaper.

The young Onslows became involved with the three sons of Lady Lovelace born when she had been Mrs Jenkins: Edward

Boycott (b. 1849), Herbert Charles (b. 1851), and Atherton Edward (b. 1859). The Clandon visitor's book shows the signatures of "Mr E. Jenkins and Lady Margaret Jenkins". On the evening of the 22nd April 1871, Hillier writes in his diary, *went to dine with Jenkins at the Mitre and to Harris's room where I met Jenkins*. Hillier had been at Oxford with Edward, who was a barrister-at-law. His brothers were colonels in the British army. All the men were acceptable to Surrey society as they bred broodmares and racehorses.

During this time, Hillier had to negotiate with Aunt Augusta, the 3rd Earl's sister. Hillier wrote *she made me exceedingly angry by her pettishness. Nothing in the house worth having but Delaroche's Napoleon, Thorwaldsen's Shepherd, Canova's bust of Napoleon and Hogarth's House of Commons, the latter I still hope to get hold of. She made me look at her absurd temple and strawberry beds.* The 3rd Earl had left most of the family collection to his sister Augusta. Two years after Augusta's death, as they were not entailed, the whole collection, which included Onslow heirlooms, were sold by auction. Gradually, the estate began to feel the pressures of Guildford's expansion and the agricultural changes. A sense of crisis developed, and on Lady's Day 1877, a family friend, Arthur Humphrey Bowles, became land agent and steered the ship safely until 1911, when the fear of Gladstone's "dreadful military spirit" became a reality.

Lord Lovelace was also struggling. His estates were by far the most important to the local economy and he was, directly or indirectly, the largest employer. His Surrey lands were also his principal source of investment capital, together with holdings in Leicestershire, Somerset, and other places. He rented out a few farmhouses in Ockham as private residences, which made little impact on improving his finances. The 1st Earl Lovelace was already seventy-three when he found himself having to cope with a major slump.

Despite financial problems, the Earl continued to live at Horsley Towers and, like many landowners, was represented in the day-to-day running of affairs by a land agent, Byron Noel, a relative. From 1875 to 1878, Ockham Park was rented out to Captain George Cockburn. As the depression bit, some of the smaller farms became managed by bailiffs because they could not be leased out at economic rents.

During this period, many farmers failed. Farms could not be let and values plummeted. Farmhouses and the cottages of farm labourers became available at bargain prices, making them attractive to town dwellers in search of a place live. More and more farmland was bought to become parklands or gardens.

The human cost of the agricultural depression was high. Traditional patterns of working were disrupted and wages continued to fall. Competition for the few remaining jobs was keen. Workers from all over Britain and Ireland struggled to find work. However, Harry continued to have work. Many displaced labourers and domestic servants fled to the cities or overseas rather than risk starving to death.

Lord Lovelace allocated several acres of land for the use of agricultural labourers, at a low rent, and gave prizes each year for the best-kept plots. He was interested in agricultural improvements, and a member of the council of the Royal Agricultural Society of England which encouraged observation and experimentation. His Lordship also gave lectures on matters of agricultural improvements and published pamphlets on the subject.

A very different person from either the 1st Earl of Lovelace or 4th Earl of Onslow, the Rev'd Charles Dodgson sat writing in a house called Chestnuts which nestled by the side of Guildford Castle. A young friend of his, Alice Liddell, wished to be entertained – and so *Alice Through the Looking Glass* was born. Three years before, on 14th August 1868, Guildfordians observed a tall, slim young man with a sensitive, refined face walking through the town. The Rev'd Charles Dodgson was searching for a house. He had been recently orphaned and was searching for a home for his six sisters.

The young don found a suitable house – the Chestnuts. It was available for a rent of £73 per annum. The ladies must have found conditions cramped, although the house contained four floors, with four rooms on each, the kitchen, sitting room, scullery, and larder were in the semi-basement. On the main floor could be found the drawing room, and across the hall, the dining room and sitting room. The top two floors housed four bedrooms each.

Immediately they had moved in, the Dodgson sisters started to do good works and their social circle widened. On 23rd July 1869, they gave their first dinner party. Among the guests was Dr Merriman, the headmaster of the Royal Grammar School. Other friendships included the Haydons, the banking family, and Mr Hulme, the surgeon. The Dodgson sisters attended a croquet party and enjoyed spending the evening with solicitor Smallpiece. On 27th December 1869, the Rev'd Dodgson took part in a theatrical performance. This was held in the "Leas", the home of another family friend, the diplomat and author William Webb Follett Synge. Among the audience were Mr and Mrs Anthony Trollope. Perhaps they were the only people to realize who the Rev'd Dodgson really was. Although he enjoyed worldwide fame, he hoped that few, beyond his little girlfriends, knew he was the famous author Lewis Carroll, and was offended if he or his works were referred to in general company.

Queen Victoria so enjoyed *Alice in Wonderland* that she commanded, "I wish to read the complete works of Mr Lewis Carroll." Her Majesty found these included books on matrix algebra, mathematical logic, and Kronecker-Capelli theorem.

Meanwhile, the local newspapers began to report sightings of a new form of transport – the high-wheel bicycle or "Penny Farthing". It first appeared in Ripley High Street in 1869, and was especially welcomed by Mrs Harriet Dibble, widow and respectable landlady of the Anchor. Harry was disgusted to see cyclists flocking into Ripley in their thousands on a Sunday.

Ripley became the Mecca for the new, athletic, young, adventurous person. Hannah was shocked to see women as well as men cycling the twenty-three miles from London along the Portsmouth Road and into the countryside, pedalling on half-macadamised roads previously used only by coaches and oxcarts. The cyclists said that "the ten mile route from the Angel Inn, Thames Ditton, along the Portsmouth Road via Ripley and on to Dorking was the best cycling highway in the world."

The Anchor Inn, with its numerous gables and roots stretching as far back as 1500, was even known to Queen Elizabeth I. In her time, fresh horses could be hired for a 1d a mile. Four centuries later, it became the favourite place for cyclists to stop and refresh themselves. Mrs Dibble was never sued for serving poisonous beer, as had the landlord of the Ship, just along the High Street.

Custom came so thick and fast that Mrs Dibble opened a "Cyclists' Visitors Book". Her two beautiful daughters became the objects of desire for every young male cyclist. Mrs Dibble gained so much in respectability that when the Ripley Girls' Friendly Society was formed in 1878, she became chairperson, with one of the Miss Onslows as President.

Harry had no time for such "contraptions", saying he preferred to go by "Shank's pony". The size of his family continued to increase, and it is not known why they moved briefly to Ockham. He did boast he was butler to Lord Lovelace for a time, but it seems unlikely – perhaps he was an indoor servant.

An event occurred that Harry took little notice of at the time, which later he thought was "heathen, the work of the very devil". It took place in 1879, in St John's, Woking, where somebody carried out an experiment and cremated a horse. Harry's friend the gravedigger commented, "Why, bodies buried in Ripley churchyard soil are gone within five years, only bits of the coffin lid remind you once somebody was there."

Harry continued to tell the stories of old Surrey, including tales of ghosts. Three ghosts are supposed to haunt Loseley: a

green-coated hunter, a sallow lady, and a warrior in plate
armour, who once appeared to a kitchen maid as she was
drawing some beer in the cellar, and scared her half to death.

However, there is one lesser-known ghost. Hanging in a
passage of Loseley is a portrait of a small, gracious, elderly lady
with dark hair. Her name is not known, but she may be Eliza,
the daughter of Colonel Sir Claud Hagart Alexander of
Ballochmyle. In 1874, he built Eastbury Manor, Compton – the
same year that James Molyneux died. His bachelor son William
inherited the estate. Surprisingly, three years later, at the age of
forty-two, he built a nursery wing on the south side of the house.
It remained empty. William never married, and never saw his
children playing there.

Many years later, an elderly Scottish friend of Sir Claud came
to stay. The guest said, "I see you have a picture of great-great-
grandmother Eliza in the passage by the bathroom. We have a
full-sized portrait of her in our bedroom." Did William
Molyneux show Eliza around Loseley hoping . . . ? We shall
never know, but if he did suffer a disappointment, he managed
to live a worthwhile life. The More-Molyneuxs owned
Arlington Manor Farm, and William formed Arlington Parish
Council. He grew palm trees in his splendid gardens, and in
1894, built Arlington Church.

During the 1870s, a man who would annoy Harry by taking
on many of the responsibilities of the great landowners, Henry
Peak, continued to build up his practice as an architect-surveyor.
He was involved in constructing a new house on the site of
Stoughton Place, to the north of the centre of Guildford. The
family were extinct, but for some twenty generations had been
powerful lords of the manor. Members of the family lay in the
vault of Stoughton Chapel in the parish church of Emmanuel,
near the Wooden Bridge Inn where, many years later, the young
Rolling Stones and Eric Clapton would perform.

On 17th October 1887, when Mr Peak was engaged in
working in the vault, he came across the decaying pieces of an

elm coffin, the small end covered in crimson velvet with expensive trimmings. The brass mountings included a raised crest of a lion passant in brass, but the massive coffin handles had fallen off. Fixed to the top of the coffin was a brass plate:

'Future Praeterites
Jonathan Harris Turner
Armge
Obit Jan 27. 1737
Annus Agent s 33'.

Close by in a coffin covered,

Mrs Margaret Turner
Relict of Nicholas Turner
Of Stoke in the County of Surrey, Esq.,
Died Sep the 30 1734
In the fiftieth year of her age.

The Turners were the successors to the Stoughtons. Mr Peak closed the vault and left the Turners to their slumbers. When he entered the Guildhall council chamber, he walked passed a carved chalk fireplace. It had been there ever since the end of the 1600s, when the old house had been pulled down. It was all that remained of a once-great and powerful family.

Henry Peak, like Harry, loved southwest Surrey. He wrote in his diary *and what more glorious than to ramble to the Downs by Merrow and at Newlands Corner, or more bounteous than the nearer walk by the river-side to St Catherine's, or to Loseley Park, and the way to Compton and up to the Hog's Back and so return to the town by the old or new road as fancy might dictate.*

CHAPTER FOUR

The 1880s

A Time of Change

The "Great Blizzard" was the worst Harry ever known. It occurred on 18th January 1881. Snow fell thickly, hour after hour, winds reached gale force, gusting to more than 60 mph. Shops were forced to close, vehicles buried, a train came off its tracks, and – not seen for many a generation – skaters glided on the Bolder Mere, the strange lake close to Wisley Gardens. The Met Office announced that "the cause of the snowstorm is a deep pressure system which joins a battle between warmer Atlantic air and bitterly cold continental air." As today, nobody bothered to listen to them. They were all too busy complaining and repairing the damage.

While the storm blew, Harry was tucked away in 18 Grove Heath with Hannah, together with Montague, now sixteen years old, and fourteen-year-old Harry. They were both farm labourers. Martha, twelve, Ada, ten, Percy, six (born in Ockham), and Louisa, four, were scholars at Ripley village school. Hannah had two toddlers as well to look after: Herbert, three, and one-year-old Ernest. Later, both children appear in the school lists.

In the 1881 census, Harry appears as thirty-eight years of age, farm stockman at Bridgefoot Farm. As the blizzard abated, he spent the next few days calming animals down, repairing fences, and searching for feed for them.

Harry thought the name "Grove Heath" probably derived

from a small wood on the heath, or it may have been the home
of a 13th-century gentleman whom the Vicar told him was a
Richard de la Grave. The cottage Harry lived in was built in the
1820s. All the little homes were unusually built closely together
and were of 17th- and 19th-century origin. The hamlet lay within
the parish of Ripley on outlying land. It felt it possessed a separate identity from Ripley itself, and possessed none of the
village's communal facilities except for the Jovial Sailor Inn,
which still stands on the Portsmouth Road. The ancient foot-
path linking the hamlet with Ripley is now a private road. Most
mornings, it was trod by thirty pairs of feet as the children of
Grove Heath trudged unwillingly to school.

By this time, the old custom of paying the workforce partly
in kind (which often included a beer allowance) was giving way
to a full money wage. A farm labourer earned about 12s a week.
Harry, as a skilled stockman, would expect to earn 1s or 2s per
week more than an ordinary day labourer, partly because he
worked on Sundays and because of his extra responsibilities.
When he became an old man, he would be lucky to earn 7/6d a
week. A sampler hung on the wall of his cottage, worked by
Hannah – Proverbs 12:10: *A righteous man cares for the needs of his
animals*. Being with them for at least twelve hours a day, he cared
for them almost as much as he did for his own children.

Harry stayed with his animals whenever they became sick or
gave birth. Like many stockmen, he prided himself on
possessing his own remedies, such as celandine to clear worms
or horehound to cure a cold, but Harry possessed his own secret
brew which could be used only in emergencies. If it did not kill
the animal, it would cure all known illnesses. The formula is not
known. He took it to the grave with him.

When it was time for the animals to go to slaughter, Harry
went with them. He said, "They know, you know. Animals are
put by God on this earth for the benefit of man, but cruelty is
an abomination to the Lord." Like most Victorians, he thought
animals did not have souls. However, there was growing aware-

ness that they possessed feelings. Many people felt it was wrong to eat other living creatures. His role model, Lord Lovelace, was a vegetarian who also abhorred alcohol and tobacco. On 30th September 1847, the Vegetarian Society was formed with the aims of *supporting, representing and increasing the number of vegetarians in the United Kingdom*. Harry heard of the Society, but continued to enjoy his Sunday roast and glass of stout.

Unlike many people in the 19th century, he did not agree with the Rev'd William Cowherd of the Bible Christian Society, who said, "If God had meant us to eat meat then it would have come to us in edible form, as is the ripened fruit." In 1895, Mrs E. W. Bowditch produced her book of vegetarian recipes. In 1899, Isaac Pitman opened his Vegetarian Hotel in Birmingham.

In 1875, a Royal Commission was set up. On its recommendation, legislation was put into place to control cruelty to animals. In 1876, the Cruelty to Animals Act was passed, which stipulated that researchers would be prosecuted for cruelty unless they conformed to its provisions – an experiment involving the infliction of pain upon animals could only be conducted when the proposed experiments were essential to save or prolong human life. The animals must be anaesthetised, used only once (though several procedures regarded as the same experiment were permitted), and killed as soon as the study was over. The Act was applicable to vertebrate animals only, and was considered to be "infamous but well-named".

On 2nd December 1875, the National Antivivisection Society was formed with the support of many notable people, such as Queen Victoria and Lord Shaftesbury. In 1888, the Queen was photographed sitting in her carriage cuddling Marco, her pet Pomeranian. However, many of her subjects were less kindly disposed towards animals.

Vivisection continued under the control of the Home Office, who awarded licenses for experiments which continued in secret laboratories, hidden with no public access, even to fellow professionals or members of Parliament. As a boy, Harry had walked through the Shambles at Guildford and saw for himself the careless cruelty of the slaughterhouse men. Pigs and chickens were slaughtered in backyards, blood flowing across pavements.

Many animals were killed prior to Christmas, but during December and January, they would be kept inside. As winter drew on, the increasingly muddy conditions gave overworked horses a rest, but it depended on the usefulness of the animal how well it would be cared for. Milking cows, beef cows, heifers, or bullocks were given root crops such as swedes or turnips. If there had been a good harvest, they munched hay. Sheep were confined in hurdles and moved on each day. A back fence was put in place so the animals could not move back on to "foul land". Every morning, they went onto a new stretch of pasture.

During this slack time, stockmen cleaned out stockyards, repaired fencing and implements, and began preparations for the coming of spring. However, like pigs and country folk everywhere, Harry sensed when winter began creeping away. He recalled Miss Jekyll writing *there is always in February some one day, at least, when one smells the yet distant, but surely coming, summer*. It was at such times when Harry saw his piglets start to gambol around. He would leave them alone, allowing them to roam in the woods snuffling for acorns and seeds, fattening themselves up for November and the slaughterman's knife.

The routine of the farm year continued the same, year in and year out: January, spread manure fields; February, fill dyke, hedging, and ditching; March, sow grain; April, sow root crops; summer months are harvest time. While Harry worked hard, for some people, there was more time for leisure.

Cyclists continued to come into Ripley. In 1885, Harry was pleased when the Rev'd Henry Hooper, curate of Send and Ripley (Vicar of Ripley 1879–95), started regular services for cyclists. He soon became known as "the cyclists' vicar". A concert for the benefit of the poor of Ripley was held in the National School on Saturday, 16th November 1889, doors opening at 7 p.m. During the evening, the Rev'd Hooper was presented with the Cyclists' Testimonial. He also received a pen-and-ink portrait of himself, and an oak writing table with a foldaway Hammond typewriter. Major Knox-Holmes, a much respected older cyclist, was in the chair, and performed a song accompanied by Mr Herbert E. Crimp. The Major had taken to cycle racing at the age of seventy-five. Four years later, together with a younger man, he set national track records from twenty-six to thirty miles on a tandem tricycle. The evening closed with supper and a rendering of *God Save the Queen*. Tickets were 2s, 1s, or 6d each.

The Rev'd Hooper found that attendance at service some-times fell short. Some cyclists preferred to digest Mrs Dibble's excellent lunch with a drink and a postprandial pipe. However, on one occasion, he was delighted when 126 cyclists, including a party of visiting Americans, attended service. The Rev'd Hooper certainly did not approve of taking pleasure on Sunday, but felt that if people were going to ignore the Sabbath, he might as well put on a service for them.

In the same year, on 26th March 1885, a cry could be heard from the genteel inhabitants of St John's: "A woman is to be burned!" The body of Mrs Pickersgill, a member of the Cremation Society, was being conveyed from Woking station to the suburb. It would be the first legal cremation to take place in Britain. A small plot of land had been purchased in 1878, *in a secluded part of Woking parish (St John's) admirably suited for the purpose, and sufficiently remote from habitations . . .* The Society built its crematorium in a plain, utilitarian style. In 1899, they replaced it with a redbrick building with stone dressings, in the style of the early 13th century, surrounded by lawns and flowerbeds.

Many people had re-examined the biblical phase *for dust thou art and unto dust thou shalt return*, and approved of the scheme. Harry did not. In 1879, the Home Secretary, Mr R. A. Cross, said he was in favour of cremation, but Lord Onslow, together with the vicars of St John's and Woking, along with many residents, did not. They asked, "What will happen to house prices?"

Woking had grown up fast. In less than a generation, it had become a modern commuter town. The town's centre of gravity shifted to the railway station, making it easily accessible for commuters. Thousands arrived. Rows of "like-minded" houses clustered together all over the parish. The population also increased through an influx of Asians. Harry and his kind never envisaged an Asian community taking root less than twenty miles from Ripley.

Many came to Woking because of the initiative of Dr Gottlieb Wilhelm Leitner, a Hungarian Jew who had become enthralled with the East. A linguist, orientalist, and educationalist, he searched for a suitable site to set up an institute to study Asian languages, culture, and history. In the spring of 1884, he established a college for Oriental studies on the site of the defunct Royal Dramatic College. Dr Leitner hoped the Institute would be a place of study for those Asians who lived in Europe and wished to enter the learned professions. He hoped the Institute would be granted university status. He observed, "there is no place in the world where the Institute and its publications are least known than in Surrey."

It was Dr Leitner who founded the Shah Jehan Mosque, which was one of the first to be built in western Europe. The land was bought with funds donated by the Nizam of Hyderabad, and the mosque with a donation from the Begum Shah Jahan of Bhopal. It remains a symbol of tolerance, still being visited by numerous Muslim dignitaries and diplomats. When Queen Victoria stayed at Windsor Castle, her Indian attendants worshipped in the little mosque.

Harry knew that Her Majesty employed Indian servants. However, he was upset when he learned, in 1899, of the appearance, under the grey skies of Woking, of a dignified little building built *beside the down-line*. The Shah Jehan Mosque *was as pretty as the Brighton Pavilion*. Such was the appeal of the East that Mr Maling Grant, an indigo planter from Bengal, gave his main address in the 1906 *Who's Who* as Bhagalpur, Bengal, but continued bringing up his family discreetly at Sendhurst Grange, Woking.

Presumably, Miss Jekyll, living in Godalming, knew little of Surrey's Asian community. By 1881, she was sharing Munstead House near Godalming with her mother, grateful that the *years of homesickness* were over. She had written to a friend, the artist George Leslie, *I only hated Berkshire because it was not Surrey and it was chalk and not sand.* Mrs Jekyll chose to live in Munstead House as it was only a carriage-drive away from their old home at Bramley. Godalming station was close by and her daughter could arrive at Waterloo station in less than an hour.

On Miss Jekyll's arrival at Munstead House, she quickly transposed plants and fruit trees from the garden at Wargrave. By 1880, her mother's garden was good enough to be inspected by visitors. They included such eminent horticulturists as Harry Mangles, the rhododendron expert, the writer William Robinson, and the rose grower Dean Samuel Reynold Hole, later Dean of Rochester Cathedral and a founder of the Golders Green Crematorium.

Gertrude was one of the contributors to William Robinson's journal *The Garden: An Illustrated Weekly Journal of Horticulture in all its Branches*. Articles included such subjects as the kitchen garden's need of water, the yellow pine, the pathway, wall-flowers, and hardy cacti. Details were given of Highclere Castle's park and gardens, the great garden at Kew, and others in New York, Germany, and Rome. Announcements were made of forthcoming events, such as a dinner for the Gardeners' Royal Benevolent Institute and a report of a meeting, in the Conservatory at Kensington, of the Royal Horticultural Society.

Harry, of course, never read *The Garden*. It was not meant for his kind of person. Modern trends did not interest him. His idea of a cottage garden was very different from Miss Jekyll's. She divided her land into rooms. Harry, on the other hand, grew a few flowers and rows and rows of vegetables, swinging above them lines of dead starlings as a warning to other birds.

By 1881, Gertrude Jekyll's prestige as a "plants woman" was rising so high that she was asked to be a judge at the Great Spring Show. This took place in the RHS gardens at Kensington. In 1913, it moved into the grounds of Chelsea Hospital. Harry did not know then that towards the end of his life, "Chelsea" would become the focal point of his year.

This was also the year which brought Miss Jekyll into contact with influences which affected the style of her gardens. Herbert, her youngest brother, married Agnes, the daughter of William Graham, wine importer, MP for Glasgow, and patron of many of the pre-Raphaelites, such as the artists Dante Gabriel Rossetti and Edward Burne-Jones. The discussions which resulted from this marriage made Miss Jekyll grow closer to her friend Hercule Brabazon, who himself was an impressionist artist much influenced by the pre-Raphaelite movement. She said how grateful she was to him "for . . . sympathetic guidance and encouragement in the observation and study of colour and beauty".

Most of all, Miss Jekyll loved to harness Bessie and trot the dogcart along the Surrey lanes through arches of overhanging elms. Despite her short-sightedness, she noted everything – flowers growing on the side of the lane, and mosses and pebbles under the hedgerows, as well the great houses and cottages which blended in so well they seemed to have been there forever.

It was on one particularly sunny afternoon in 1889 that Miss Jekyll did as she so often did: took tea with Mr Harry Mangles of Littleworth. As they sat talking over the teacups, *the silver kettle and the conversation reflecting rhododendrons*, the clanking of a bicycle disturbed the peace. A tinkling bell announced the arrival of a young man, Mr Edwin Lutyens. He was a twenty-year-old architect designing cottages for Mr Mangles. Miss Jekyll did not talk very much to the young man, but when she was about to leave, with one step placed on the foot of her pony cart and holding the reins in her hand, Miss Jekyll turned round and said to young Lutyens, "take tea with me, next Saturday." The fifty-year-old spinster and the young man became lifelong friends. It was this friendship which would change their lives forever, as well as the Surrey landscape.

At this time, the young 4th Earl of Onslow began to want to follow in his family tradition of public service. In 1880, Queen Victoria appointed him as Lord-in-Waiting under Disraeli. Later, he held this role under Lord Salisbury. It was a non-political appointment, but Onslow could act on the Queen's behalf, such as looking after and welcoming visiting dignitaries (when the President of the United States, Barack Obama, arrived one day earlier than planned from his visit to Ireland, he was greeted by Lord-in-Waiting Viscount Brookeborough).

Hillier proved to be an able man, and government appointments soon followed: Undersecretary for the Colonies, Undersecretary of State for India, Privy Councillor, and President of the Board of Agriculture. In the year of Queen Victoria's Golden Jubilee in 1887, he was involved with the organisation of the First Colonial Conference *with the aim of creating closer ties between the colonies and the United Kingdom*. One hundred delegates attended from the Colonies and the United Kingdom. A representative from India was not present. The Prime Minister, Lord Salisbury, was in the chair, and Hillier acted as Vice-President. He invited one particularly difficult Australian delegate to join him for dinner at 8:15 p.m. in Richmond Terrace, Whitehall. He tactfully said, "Lady Onslow will be unable to be present." Hillier decided the man was "no ordinary colonial" and discussed an emotive subject with him: *to extend the Queen's title to Queen of the United Kingdom of Great Britain, Ireland and the Colonies, and all Dependencies thereof, and Empress of India.*

Hillier observed that "the world is a dangerous place, not because of those who do evil, but because of those who do nothing." As a parish constable, Harry may have agreed with

His Lordship. Certainly, the temperance movement was strong in Surrey. On 4th August 1880, Hillier laid the foundation stone for the Royal Arms Coffee Tavern and Temperance Hotel. The Guildford Institute occupied the upper floors, and is still in the same place today, on the corner of Ward Street and North Street, Guildford.

Guildford had much to attract city dwellers, who discovered they could travel to the comfortable market town in less than an hour. The closeness of London, and articles in magazines such as *The Lady*, meant that many of Lord Onslow's and Lord Lovelace's tenant farmers' wives aped the elegance of ladies, dressing in a style most unsuited for work in a farmer's kitchen. Many farmers, who were dependent on their wives, started to produce less. Some even stopped producing butter and cheese, and sent it as milk to London by rail.

However, in 1882, Mr Gate, the owner of the grocer's shop at 20 High Street, Guildford, died. His sons Charles Arthur and Leonard took over the running of his business, which included the local franchise for the largest distributor of wines and spirits in the country. The brothers also sold beer. In 1885, they joined the temperance movement. One day, much to the horror of most Guildfordians, they poured their alcoholic stock into the gutters of the High Street, and became a dairy. The brothers bought milk from local farmers and used a milk separator to separate the cream from the whey. They sold the cream in little brown jugs featuring a picture of a cow looking through a gate, and sold the skimmed milk back to the farmers for pig feed. Even Queen Victoria consumed "Cow and Gate Milk". Hannah enjoyed it; Harry "never touched the stuff". Eventually, the company developed into the West Surrey Central Dairy Company, producing pure English dried milk.

By 1881, Arthur Lambert's second son Walter was the tenant of Bridgefoot Farm. His wife Sarah was unlikely to act above her station. She would have been expected to run the household, care for her children, manage indoor servants, and feed, clothe, and find tasks for any children of relatives who were farmed out to their more prosperous relations.

There was also the little maid-of-all-work. She would have been responsible for all the chores, inside and outside, including carrying coals and bathwater to the top of the house, and lighting the fires. A good servant was expected to light the fire with six pieces of kindling. Lambert may have reduced his dairy herd and turned to arable farming, but during the 1880s, his landholding decreased by more than a hundred acres.

It was not only the wives of the older farmers who noted the ladylike behaviour of the young women. The writer Richard Jefferies, in 1880, noted whiteness of hands and rings on every finger. He enquired, *has not some of the old stubborn spirit of earnest work and careful prudence gone with the advent of the piano and the oil painting?* These were some of the changes which added to the pressures on Hillier and increased his financial problems, together with the start of a family. In 1876, his heir Richard, Viscount Onslow, was born, followed (in 1881) by a daughter, Gwendolen.

During this period, Harry also would have needed his children to earn "something". Hillier came to a decision – a difficult one for an aristocrat – he must find a salaried position. At the age of thirty-four, the 4th Earl of Onslow became one of the youngest ever governors of New Zealand. It is in this role that southwest Surrey most remembers him. Hillier improved the relations between settlers and Maori, who still say, "The Lords Onslow have a special place in our hearts."

During the couple's time in New Zealand, another two children were born: in 1885, Dorothy, and five years later (in 1890), Huia. Queen Victoria commanded that the little boy should be christened Victor Alexander. An uncle suggested "Herbert". His parents added a fourth name: Huia, a Maori name "for an almost extinct bird and a precious treasure". At ten months old, Huia (as he would be known by) was received into the Ngati

Huia tribe. The chief was followed by the Onslow's terrified nanny. The baby did not utter a sound, but watched the proceedings in wide-eyed wonderment.

In 1892, despite *not possessing flair or flamboyance*, the Onslows successfully returned to Clandon. In 1887, he was created a Knight Commander of St Michael and St George (KCMG). Two years later, he became a GCMG (a knight of the Grand Cross). This is an order of chivalry given for extraordinary service in a foreign country. The couple brought with them "Hinemhi" (a Maori meeting house) and paid £50 to the son of a chief for it. It had been buried deep under the debris of a volcanic eruption and needed to be dug out. As a constant reminder of their four happy "New Zealand years", Lord and Lady Onslow, watching from Clandon Park, saw who came to visit "Hinemhi".

On his return to Surrey, Hillier continued in politics. He chaired numerous committees in the House of Lords, remembering at all times Disraeli's advice: "Onslow, always shut a door." A shrewd politician, he knew doors have ears. Even though he was so busy, Lord Onslow kept firm control of the management of his estates. He worked with local solicitors Smallpiece and Merriman, and land agents Norman and Appleby. His estates were widespread, and included tenant farms in Slyfield, Stoke-next-Guildford, Burpham, Worplesdon, and Woking, as well as farms in Norfolk and Berkshire, and lands in London.

Lord Onslow also felt the need to improve the plight of agricultural labourers. In 1885, in conjunction with the Duke of Westminster, he became honorary secretary to the *Land and Glebe Owners Association for the Voluntary Extension of the Allotment System*. His books on the subject included *Landlords and Allotments: The History and Present Condition of the Allotment System* and reports "to inquire into and report on the departmental committee appointed by the Board of Agriculture and Fisheries." He collected a mass of statistics and opinions from landlords and clergy all over the country, and was a member of the Royal Statistical Society, along with Florence Nightingale and Charles Babbage. In 1905–6, he became President (two prime ministers have also enjoyed this position: William Ewart Gladstone and Harold Wilson). In 1886, he wrote a letter addressed to his tenantry: *The Immediate Future of Agriculture.*

The Onslows entertained a great deal. Florence kept a book in which she noted the name of her guests for luncheons, dinners, regular Parliamentary dinners, and Cabinet luncheons. The Onslows enjoyed after-theatre supper parties and, among other things, children's tea parties. On Hillier's birthday in 1883, six courses were served, including *Consommé à la Reine, Sole Colbert, and Côtelettes d'Agneau.* The chef was a Neapolitan, Signor di Luca. Hillier loathed garlic, but occasionally a little was sneaked into the food. If detected, Hillier went into a fury and scribbled on a menu card *Bannissez l'ail de la cuisine!* and despatched it immediately to the kitchen. On reading it, Signor di Luca would fly into a screaming fit.

Apart from political appointments, Onslow had several senior local responsibilities, which included being High Steward of Guildford. This has been defined as "an office of some dignity and some influence but with no practical duties or emoluments". The High Steward does, however, present a plum cake to any member of the Royal family when they visit Guildford. Sensing the increase of trade flowing into Guildford as "Lord of the Manor", in July 1882, Hillier commissioned a bridge to be built from the High Street over the River Wey. As it was on his land, he agreed to pay for the Onslow Bridge, but asked the Corporation to contribute £6,500 towards the cost.

The shopkeepers were outraged. His Lordship was correct in saying people could come into Guildford easily; it was equally true that Guildfordians could cross the bridge to patronize the shops in the nearby towns of Godalming and Haslemere.

A poster appeared:

OPENING OF THE NEW BRIDGE
*Rejoice O ye ratepayers, That £6,500 of your money has gone to
obligate a Noble Lord Rejoice O ye tradesmen That it is not spent
in the town, but at the Civil Service Stores, Therefore shut up your
shops and be merry, saith the Mayor.*

Lady Florence opened the Onslow Bridge in 1882. A notice
says, *Erected by William Hillier Onslow, 4ᵗʰ Earl of Onslow, High
Steward of Guildford.*

The ratepayers were mortified as the Borough Council
continued spending their money. In 1888, it acquired lands
around the castle and started to plan a pleasure park. Dr G. C.
Williamson, in his book *Olden Times: Side-lights of the History of
a Quaint Old Town*, mentions that when the Castle grounds were
bought by the Corporation in 1886, landscape gardeners were
asked to submit plans to lay out the space. One suggestion was
that the ugly ruin (castle) in the centre of the grounds be
removed, and in its place should be built a "light iron band-
stand, painted green and picked with gold".

A stone column nearby provided the first gaslight for the
town (Clandon Park already possessed gas lighting). In 1889,
the corporation purchased, from James Budgett, Stoke Park
together with its woodlands, ice-house, manor and walled garden.
Throughout much of the 18ᵗʰ century and into the 19ᵗʰ century,
the estate had been the property of the Onslows until Hillier
sold it in 1879 to Mr Budgett. As the town grew, the Park
became known as "the lungs of Guildford".

In the same year, in Castle Street in the centre of the town,
one of the first public swimming baths in the country was
opened. In 1885, domestic refuse began to be collected regularly by horse-drawn carts, and in Clive Road, the first council
house appeared. Between 1889 and 1895, an advanced major
sewerage scheme was introduced into the town. The world of
the medieval alleyway was over. The town people started to
mutter, "Surely, we should be a City." Charles Combe of

Cobham Park found himself having to write, on 11th April 1884, *The Lord Lieutenant (Lord Lovelace) has been kind enough to say that he will nominate me Deputy Lieutenant and asks me to send him a statement of my qualifications to Richard Wyatt Clerk to the Justice of the Peace for Surrey.*

There was another development which shocked some of the inhabitants of Guildford. In 1509, Guildfordian Robert Beckingham left a foundation for the formation of a free grammar school for the "towne of Guildford". However, by 1888, it was in financial difficulties, nearly closing. Fortunately, efforts were made to save it and it became a day school.

On 25th April 1887, the Church Schools Company opened a progressive high school for girls in Haydon Place, with the principle aim of *educating young women in the Christian virtues, especially Anglican principles.* It wished to become the feminine counterpart to the reformed boys' public schools, and hoped its girls would possess wider horizons than just following careers as governesses. However, when the first headmistress, Miss Agnes Morton, opened the school, she was greeted by the caretaker with "there ain't no one come yet." By the end of the first week, two pupils had joined, and with support from the Church Schools Company, it acquired more pupils. In 1893, a new school was constructed which also became a day school. By the 1920s, 200 girls were being educated in Guildford High School.

Despite the changes to education and those made by the Borough Council, Surrey remained "full of sporting thrills". Hunting in the county is an ancient institution. It is recorded that in 1750, Mr Gobsall of Bermondsey kept hounds. The first recorded pack of foxhounds was kennelled at Lovell Grove, Croydon, where the Earl of Onslow was living in 1735. Green is the traditional old Surrey colour, and traces its history to the colour of dress worn by City merchants in the 1860s. There is a record of the hounds killing a fox close to Croydon station, and as the century continued, it was noted that foxes became scarcer in the area.

R. S. Surtees' Cockney grocer Mr Jorrocks hunted with the Surrey Foxhounds. In 1853, a Mr Byron began to hunt on his pony with the Old Surrey Hounds *since which time this hunting country, then as wild as it is possible to imagine, has been largely over run by the enterprising builder.*

The Earl of Lovelace complained about the 1880–81 season that "in the more rural area of Surrey, meets are being unequally distributed and that my particular district has been hardly hunted upon." At the end of the 19th century, fox hunting was considered essential to landowners and farmers. They were seen as vermin and a threat to a man's livelihood. Harry reported immediately any sightings. He said, "A fox will take the last bird. A cat will always be master, but a large dog can be a vicious enemy." He thought the hunt went out at the wrong time. "Reynard hunts before dawn and appears in the late evening and an old fox may wear out the hunt. It can run three-and-a-half to four hours, easily."

An old woman complained to the Surrey Union Hunt that "a fox killed one of my geese. It bit its head right off. Please recompense me as it is the duty of the hunt to control foxes. A coven has been seen playing on the common."

On 7th March 1885, one master, a Colonel Blake, declared that "in forty days of hunting, eighteen foxes had been killed, fourteen run to ground. There were seven blank days and four stopped by frost," and added, "Sir, hunting three days a week is simply a matter of money."

In 1889, the Surrey Hunt agreed that subscriptions should be raised to £10 a year. This would give membership of the hunt and permission to wear the Hunt button which had previously been allowed only by express invitation of the Master. Another master extolled, "Wear pink, Sir. Red coats are forgiven indiscretions; black coats, none."

Throughout Surrey inns for many years, the old folksong continued to be sung, commemorating the gruesome find which the Surrey Union Hunt made in January 1834:

It was Hankey the Squire as I have heard say
Who rode out a-hunting on one Saturday.
They hunted all day, but nothing they found
But poor murdered woman, laid on the cold ground. . . .
No father, No mother, nor no friend I'm told
Come to see that poor creature put under the mould. . . .

Fox-hunting people are usually racing people, and most of the great English racehorses have been, and will be, seen at Sandown, Esher's racecourse. Eric Parker described it as *the long flank of a green hill, the white pavilion under dark pines, and the curving course picked out with fresh painted railings and green canvas.* Sadly, racing is no longer seen on Merrow Downs, even with harriers. They have been built upon long ago, but Sandown still remembers the time, in July 1886, when the banker and friend of the Prince of Wales, Leopold de Rothschild, donated £10,000 prize money for the Eclipse Stakes, a 2,018-metre flat race. It was won by the favourite, Bendigo, for the racehorse breeder Mr Hedworth Barclay – the first time any horse had won such a sum.

"Ordinary people" often enjoyed racing, but by the end of the 19th century, could spend their newfound leisure in various ways. It was the Grove family who were responsible for the upkeep of the Wey Navigation Canal, its banks and locks. They said firmly, "We have nothing to do with the Worsfolds."

In 1880, the boathouse at Worsfold Gates started hiring out all sorts of pleasure craft – skiffs, punts, and canoes. Many of the Sunday School or Girls Friendly Society outings consisted of a trip on the river. Other pleasure craft were allowed to use the canal after payment of a toll. The collection was yet a further task in the life of the canal worker. Four generations of the Grove family worked on the canal. Two of them were master carpenters based at Worsfold Gates. In the workshop, they not only prepared all the wood needed, but made the metalwork too, including nuts and bolts. There was always a gluepot bubbling on the stove, and the smell permeated everywhere.

Just before Christmas 1882, a new tombstone appeared in Ripley churchyard. It read *George, 26 years. Sexton of this parish died 14ᵗʰ December 1882 aged 76.* Five years later, another inscription is added: *Elizabeth wife of the above died 15ᵗʰ February, 1887 aged 77.*

So, Harry found himself taking on the full responsibility of being the sexton of the parish of St Mary Magdalene, Ripley. Apart from Hannah, he had nobody to rely on but himself.

CHAPTER FIVE

The 1890s

A Mauve Decade and a Time to Say Farewell

In the 1890s, mauve became the colour of fashion. A young man of eighteen discovered, accidentally, an alkaline dye. He called it "mauve". This became the colour that "one must wear". Even an agricultural worker's wife like Hannah wore a "little something in mauve". The 1891 census shows Harry, 50, and Hannah, 52, still living in Grove Heath. As an ageing man, Harry would be earning less now. A baby born in Surrey during the 1840s would expect to live for another fifty years. Nevertheless, they still had children to support: Ernest, eleven, Florence, nine, Edmund, eight, and Arthur, six. Ernest appears in the school lists. Louise, fourteen, is still at home, but there is no employment given for her. Herbert, thirteen, and Percy, sixteen, are agricultural labourers. Percy is the only child to be "born in Ockham". There is a family tradition that Harry was employed as Lord Lovelace's butler at Ockham Park. This is unlikely, but perhaps for a short time he may have been an indoor servant. Other children are listed in the census. Ernest, Florence, and Edmund appear in the Ripley school lists. By this time, the older children had left home. If anything should happen to Harry or Hannah, then the grownup children would take care of the younger ones. However, life remained the same. Live eels, caught in the River Wey, still wriggled from hooks in the kitchen. Hannah continued to feel pride in her kitchen range, rubbing it shiny black with lead polish. She enjoyed her children's pleasure when they went carol singing and received a silver three-penny piece. On the other hand, she felt great concern when a child was chased away, caught paddling in the horse trough, and losing a shoe which must be replaced. Most of all, Hannah enjoyed joining in the village laughter when a volunteer fireman fell into the farm midden (dunghill).

All the children's births appeared in Harry's great Bible, together with family funerals. Hidden between its pages was a silken, screen-printed portrait of the Great Queen-Empress. This appeared in 1897, with the *London Illustrated News*, to celebrate the Diamond Jubilee. On 22nd June, a national holiday was granted and an extra week in August added to the summer holiday. The Ripley schoolmaster recorded in the logbook, "the children from the school joined in the Jubilee Procession and had their photographs taken." Florence remembered it all her life. She told her granddaughter, "You know that school had been open for ten years when the old Queen came to the throne." One young man said he remembered the Queen's Diamond Jubilee because "I was given my first bicycle and rode from North London to take dinner at the Anchor, missing Mrs Dibble not being around."

In the Bible, there was a special entry for the birth of Harry's favourite daughter, Ada. She did well. By 1891, her father was very proud of his twenty-year-old daughter. She had left home, refusing the offer of becoming a school monitor and thus on the way to becoming a schoolmistress. At ten years of age, Ada had "gone into service" in Ripley, rising from being Mrs Willett's parlour maid to that of lady's maid. As the nineties came to an end, Ada's gentleman died. Mrs Willett took her nine daughters and tenth child, a son, to Eastbourne. Ada went too. The family appointed her housekeeper. "Worsfold" was now a modern, independent young woman with staff under her. She enjoyed good wages and, unlike her namesake, managed her financial affairs well. Every Sunday, she attended Morning

Worship with "her" family. As they entered the parish church of St Mary's, they were greeted by a carved head thought to be that of the mason who carved it. During the sermon, Ada's eye sometimes wandered to the Royal Coat of Arms of George III and the tomb of Henry Lushington, who died in 1763, a survivor of the Black Hole of Calcutta in 1756.

On the evening of Sunday, 24th July 1891, a serious disturbance took place in the town centre. Ada and Mrs Willett, together with all classes of Eastbourne's 34,000 inhabitants, were shocked at the serious injury caused to the town and its interests as a seaside resort when the Salvation Army, *unseemingly disregarding the law, ignored the ban on processions with bands on Sundays*. Nine Salvationists were committed for trial.

Now called "Miss Worsfold" by "her family", Ada loved the sea and decided on her "Sundays off" to explore Sussex. She did so with the help of a new safety bicycle. As billowing skirts were unsuitable, even dangerous, she went into the town centre and purchased "bloomers" (a divided skirt), and also a straw boater. Mrs Willett was shocked, her daughters delighted, and the son shaken. Through cycling, Ada met other strong-minded young women and became sympathetic to the suffragette movement without getting involved. Harry and Hannah, in horror, realized they had produced a "new woman". Ada stressed to her parents that "the pinkness of my complexion is due only to fresh air and exercise, not mascara and lipstick!" These were so favoured at the time by American women. When Mrs Willett died, she left Ada "a little something". None of the children married. Each one left her a small amount. The son was the last to die. He left to "Miss Ada Worsfold, our family housekeeper" the rest of the estate. Subsequently, Ada married the son's good-looking young secretary and retired to Pevensey. She lived to be over ninety. He died at fifty-two.

As with most of the village girls, Harry's daughters entered "service", but none did as well as Ada. There was plenty of work available for them. Even a lower-middle-class family had a maid-of-all-work, and a middle-class home would have a house-keeper or cook general. Upper-middle-class homes, such as Sendholme and Sendhurst Grange, employed over twenty people each. Even a relatively small establishment, such as Bramley House, employed twelve people. Great houses like Ockham Park employed many more. Each member of staff would have their own specific tasks, uniform, place in the servants' hall, and seat in church. Meals were formal, both upstairs and below stairs. Rooms were ornately furnished, and there were few labour-saving devices. Dry tea leaves were scattered onto carpets, later to be swept up with the accumulated dust. Grates needed blacking, oil lamps filling, and elaborate meals preparing for house parties. Nevertheless, sometimes deep attachments were formed. The Gladstone's precious maid-servant, Schluter, wrote to "her family" until the day she died, long after she returned to Germany to care for her aged mother.

However, conditions were better than in 1837, when Queen Victoria came to the throne. The social historian G. M. Trevelyan wrote in *English Social History* that *the Queen's Jubilees of 1887 and 1897 were celebrated by all classes with real pride and thankfulness due in part to a sense of delivery from the conditions endured at the beginning of her reign.* . . .

By 1891, the number of inhabited houses in Byfleet, a suburb of Woking, had risen to 268 – an increase of over 200 since the beginning of the century. This was indicative of the increasing prosperity, improvements in travel, and growing independence of the people of the country. Nevertheless, the patron of Byfleet church remained HM the Queen, and the 4th Earl of Onslow the patron of Ripley church.

Men of Harry's generation felt that the aristocracy possessed *noblesse oblige* (responsibility for the lower orders), knowing how things should be done. It had been rushing through their veins for centuries. Harry disliked responsibility passing into the hands of professional, educated men like architect Henry Peak, solicitor Henry Bashall, or the Lovelace estate manager Byron

Noël. These men remained in positions of authority for many years, influencing the course of events and dealing in civil as well as church matters.

However, in Harry's world, it remained the great and the good who continued to dominate his life. In 1884, he learned and welcomed the fact that his beloved Mr Gladstone had given working men, *with a household of over £10*, the right to vote. Many "ordinary" men would now have a say in how the country was run. Harry did not. It was not for the likes of him. It certainly did not occur to him that Hannah would shock him one day by saying, "as a mother, I wish to vote." However, he would have expected that, during the Indian famine, Lord Onslow would become Undersecretary of State for India in 1895. It was the sort of thing great landowners did, but he would have been very surprised to learn, a year later, that His Lordship had become an Alderman of the new London County Council. The population of the capital had risen from just over a million at the beginning of Victoria's reign, to over six million. Control was needed. The Local Government Act came into force in 1889, and after that, many local services would be under the control of county councils, district councils, and borough councils, with elected councillors and paid, qualified administrative staff. The Surrey County Council (SCC) was created in 1889. In Harry's old age, he would be employed by them to repair the roads. Therefore, the influence of the great and the good was becoming less direct and more subtle. They improved their committee skills and learned to be effective chairpersons. Three years later, in 1899, Hillier (an excellent administrator) resigned from the SCC. He said he needed "to have more time with his family and to practise his driving four-in-hand". He wished to rival the skills of his ancestor, the 2nd Earl of Onslow.

In 1893, at the age of 88, the 1st Earl of Lovelace died. A man of great natural dignity, his deafness made him appear reserved and unapproachable. However, Harry told the Vicar of Ripley,

"I had the great honour of being addressed directly by His Lordship, and the even greater honour of being allowed to reply to him." Harry attended the Earl's funeral, on a cold day in January, together with 300 other people. Lord Lovelace lies in the mausoleum which he began to prepare some twenty years before his death. On top of the tomb remains a wreath of dead flowers, placed there by his Countess. Fifteen years later, she joined him.

Nearby, in a corner of St Martin's churchyard, stands a gazebo. Old people say that when morning service was about to begin, a choirboy was sent to watch the congregation arriving at church. When the most important people were settled, the boy signalled to Horsley Towers. As he did so, His Lordship's carriage emerged through the gates of Guildford Lodge. He entered the church making a suitably dramatic entrance.

Due to the death of Byron Noel, the 1st Earl's eldest son, it was his third child, Ralph, who became the 2nd Earl of Lovelace. His Lordship had lived in Horsley Towers, and Ockham Park remained vacant until ownership passed to Ralph. The house was in such poor condition that demolition was considered. It had been rented out from 1875 until 1878, and after a short gap, to the Dowager Countess of Norbury until the early 1890s. The house remained vacant until Ralph undertook a major and time-consuming restoration. Unlike his father, the 2nd Earl took little part in public affairs. He had assumed by royal licence his grand-mother's (Lady Annabella Byron) maiden surname of Milbanke. He was already the 13th Baron Wentworth. Ralph matriculated at University College, Oxford, but did not graduate. When he was twenty-two, he spent a year in Iceland and studied Norse literature, and climbed the Alps and a peak of the Dolomites (which still bears his name). He spoke French and German fluently, conversed in both Swiss and Tyrolean dialects, and possessed a fine knowledge of music, painting, and English literature.

After the death of Harriet Beecher Stowe, the author of *Uncle*

Tom's Cabin, Ralph spent much time defending her actions. She had written an account of his grandmother's tumultuous marriage to Lord Byron – the lies, the abandonment, the violent outbursts of temper, and the secret adulterous intrigue with a blood relation. Ralph felt his grandmother's side of the story needed to be told, especially as one of Byron's mistresses, Countess Teresa Guiccioli, had published a memoir describing his grandmother as a cold, calculating, prudish woman.

Unlike his father, the 2nd Earl of Lovelace never held a conversation with Harry. Ralph also married twice. His first marriage was on 25th August 1869, to Fanny, third daughter of Rev'd George Heriot, Vicar of St Anne's, Newcastle. They had one daughter, Ada Mary. Harry named his favourite daughter after her. The Countess died in 1878. Two years later, on 10th December 1880, Ralph married Mary Caroline, the eldest daughter of the Rt. Hon. James Stuart-Wortley. Her widowed mother, the Hon. Mrs Stuart-Wortley, came to live in Ripley House, and became one of the managers of the village school.

In 1896, she presented a new dress or suit of clothes to the children who had attended school properly for a full year. They must not have taken leave for ploughing matches, fairs, or been enticed to cover beating for the shoots taking place on the great estates. The presentation became an annual event. It was the year that the school was in danger of closing and being taken over by the School Board, as its accommodation was not considered sufficient and voluntary subscriptions were not forthcoming. When the final notice of closure was just about to be served, Mrs Wortley came to the rescue. She offered the school authorities a substantial sum of money, thus solving the problem. Mrs Wortley may have felt her efforts were indeed justified when she learned that Sydney Green had won a scholarship to Guildford Grammar School, "fully funded for three years" – but sadly, at the same time, two other children were taken to the workhouse.

Prior to the Diamond Jubilee year, discussions were held

about adding a new classroom for infants to the Ripley National School. Mrs Marshall's school (for infants) in Rose Lane was closed, as there would be enough room for all the children in the main school. The Jubilee Room, as it was called, was opened in 1898, by the Bishop of Winchester. It was paid for by a massive fundraising campaign which involved the whole village. The Hon. Treasurer, Mr J. H. Sutcliff, issued the balance sheet in 1899:

Messrs. Peak and Lunn Plans cost £12.10.0d
A rummage sale raised £20.0.0d
Donations included:

The Hon. Mrs Stuart-Wortley,	£27. 7 9d,
The Earl of Onslow,	£34. 0.0d.
Lord Rendel,	£5. 5.0d.
The Earl of Lovelace,	£26. 0.0d.
Mr Sutcliff,	£15. 15.0d.
Collection by cards, (as per list)	£51.2.0d.
The Balance Sheet shows: Paid:	£749. 2. 6d.
	Received: £749. 2. 6d.

Miss Florence Gilbert, former mistress of Mrs Marshall's school, was asked take charge of the infants. Children often joined the school as toddlers. On 6th March 1894, James A. Roach, the Master, recorded in the log book, "admitted two [children] aged three years". And a former master, Mr Lewis, recorded in 1887 that he admitted a boy aged five "who had not attended a school before".

For those who were gentlemen's sons, requiring private education, Mr R. M. Pearce opened Ripley Court School, Rose Lane, in 1897. It was a boarding school and did not cater for the village boys, but it still had an impact on Ripley. Many a local boy remembered his first job there – cleaning boots, sharpening knives, tending the lamps in the school rooms, and mowing the cricket pitch. However, he would have been over eleven years of age. In 1897, the school leaving age had been raised again, to eleven years.

Mrs Wortley's daughter Mary, who was the 2nd Countess of Lovelace, was also a woman of considerable character. As the wife of one of Surrey's greatest landowners, she took an active part in Ripley life. Like most of the gentry, the Lovelaces gave a great deal to the community. Their names headed subscription lists for the school fund, the fire brigade, and the district nurse. Their gardens were opened for the annual fete or flower festival, and on special occasions such as a jubilee or a coronation. The parish magazine frequently reported parties for school children, with a magic lantern show and a conjuror, or a Christmas tea. On the Countess's initiative, ground was given for the Ripley churchyard extension. Land was leased for the church rooms and also given to the village for the children's gardening lessons.

In 1891, when the Ripley Volunteer Fire Brigade was formed, the Countess became their first president. The firemen received a fee for each turnout, and a charge was made for putting out a fire. New equipment, books, and helmets for the men were bought with funds raised by public subscription. The list of supporters was published, with names and amounts subscribed. Extra funds were raised by the horse and engine being hired out for weddings, often to take the bridesmaids to church. Lady Lovelace insisted, even in her old age, on practising fire drill with the firemen, together with her own staff. She was always first down via the chute attached to her bedroom window, "thus showing my maids the way."

It is almost forgotten now that a grand young man came to live in Worplesdon, a village near Guildford. He was HRH Prince Albert Victor of Wales, Duke of Clarence and Avondale, grandson of the Queen and eldest son of the Prince of Wales. He was respected as a fine huntsman, but strange stories of homosexual scandals abounded. However, one thing Guildfordians knew – His Royal Highness was a first-rate shot.

On a fine day in Guildford's Bull's Head, the farmers' inn opposite Tunsgate, the Prince's gardener told Harry a strange story.
One evening, he led the Duke into a copse. He wished to show
him a strange creature caught in a rabbit trap. It was a huge,
ugly, snarling thing. The Duke shot the animal, killing it
outright. When the two men pulled it out from the undergrowth, they found it was a feral cat of unnatural, extraordinary
size. The head was massive. Even in death, its eyes were forbid-
ding. The teeth were fanglike, large and sharp, the limbs
powerful, the claws outstretched, ready to inflict terrible
wounds, but the tail was wondrous, thick and black and bushy,
still seemingly alive. The two men took the thing away, crossing
themselves as they did so, and buried it. They say even now, on
a lonely part of the Portsmouth Road, a driver sees, caught in
his headlights, a huge, black, cat-like, snarling creature with
claws outstretched. . . .

Shortly after that incident, the nation was shocked to learn
of the death of the twenty-eight-year-old. The Prince died on
the morning of Thursday, 14th January 1892, in his mother's
arms, another victim of the influenza pandemic. All business in
Guildford stopped. Shopkeepers put up their shutters. On 20th
January, crowds gathered around the steps of Holy Trinity for
his memorial service. The church was filled to overflowing. The
young Prince was much regarded. He and his fiancée, Princess
Mary of Teck, were excellent in the hunting field.

Miss Jekyll's brother, Walter, may have been also something
of a strange character. Robert Louis Stevenson borrowed his
name for his novella, *The Strange Case of Dr Jekyll and Mr Hyde*.
Like Harry, Miss Jekyll remained a country soul at heart, but
unlike him, she had always *possessed short sight of the severest kind*.
As she moved into her fifties, Miss Jekyll found her eyesight
becoming more painful and inadequate. In the summer of 1891,
her doctors advised, "You must go to Wiesbaden, to see
Professor Ferman Pagenstecher, as quickly as possible. He has
been of the greatest assistance to Queen Victoria." However, the

eminent surgeon was forced to tell Miss Jekyll, "I can arrest the decline of your eyes, but I cannot offer a cure." It must have been a great sadness for him to have to make such a diagnosis. At eighty-two, he had restored the sight of a seventy-year-old man, saying, "It is always a satisfaction if, in one's old age, one can still be of use to one's fellow men."

Gertrude Jekyll returned to Surrey feeling crippled and destroyed. It took a great deal of strength of character to change her life and give up her painting and embroidery. Many years later, she wrote, *When I was young I was hoping to be a painter, but, to my lifelong regret, I was obliged to abandon all hope of this, after a certain amount of art school work, on account of extreme and always progressive myopia.*

However, sad Gertrude Jekyll felt she knew she had the support of family, friends, and the young architect Ned Lutyens. She harnessed Bessie, and the two huddled together into her governess cart and set off along the winding lanes of west Surrey. They clip-clopped through tunnels of elms whose branches stretched cathedral-like above them, noticing the primroses growing on mossy banks, almost hidden under tidy hedgerows, patchwork fields, half-tiled houses, and cosy cottages. They absorbed it all, and together began to create the Surrey style which seems as if it has always been there, growing out of the very soil.

As young Lutyens built up his practice, Gertrude Jekyll's name became increasingly respected in horticultural circles. Unlike many 19th-century single women, she was fortunate to be financially secure and part of an intellectual circle, which her family called "Gertrude's funnies". As her mother approached eighty, she found her daughter's drive and energy too taxing. Fortunately, Mrs Jekyll had purchased a parcel of land across the road. This is where Gertrude built a home of her own, but before she did so, she created a garden, leaving a space in the centre to build her house.

During the whole of 1894, Lutyens made plans for a house

which would fit into the space. Miss Jekyll moved in to a temporary home, calling it "The Hut". The following year, Mrs Jekyll died. Her brother Herbert and his family moved into Munstead House, and fortunately for Miss Jekyll, her own home, Munstead Wood, was well on its way to completion. She had stressed to Lutyens that it must have the feel of a convent, a place where owls would feel welcome to nest in the eves *and not flop all over our beds at night and frighten us out of our wits*. She instructed that passages and windows should not let in too much light, explaining, "For those with poor sight cannot cope with glare." Most of all, Gertrude Jekyll wanted a home for her cats Pinkieboy, Mr Tabby Cat, Tittlebat, and sundry kittens. Harry did not see cats as pets. They were not welcome indoors. They were meant to catch mice, and kept "in the yard".

Miss Jekyll asked Lutyens to follow John Ruskin's advice: "good whitewashed walls and tapestry are best for walls of rooms in cold climates." In the Diamond Jubilee year of 1897, Gertrude Jekyll moved into Munstead Wood. It is one of the finest arts-and-craft houses in the country, and now Grade I listed. Emily Lutyens described her first meeting with "Bumps": *She was the most enchanting person in the loveliest cottage . . . after dinner we sat in the chimney corner. A real old chimney corner with a wood fire, and there we sat and ate almonds and drank hot elderberry wine until we were quite tipsy. . . .*

In 1897, Queen Victoria had reigned for sixty years. In her honour, the Royal Horticultural Society established the Victoria Medal of Honour (VMH). Not only was Miss Jekyll delighted to have a home of her own, but also to find that she was worthy to receive the VMH, one of the few women to do so. This is only presented to horticulturalists the Society feels deserving of special honour. Mr Wilson also accepted the VMH. Her Majesty reigned for sixty-three years. This is the maximum number of people, at any one time, that may possess the VMH.

Most dramatic of all, on 4th August 1897, Lady Emily

Bulwer-Lytton, third daughter of the 1ˢᵗ Earl of Lytton, Viceroy
of India, married Ned Lutyens. She had proposed to him two
years previously. Gertrude may have considered, like Emily's
parents, that "it was an unwise union." However, she had little
time to give the matter thought. Even though Miss Jekyll
considered herself to be "a working amateur", she was busy
"running a business". Like many Victorians, such as the author
of *Alice In Wonderland*, Lewis Carroll (Rev'd Dodgson), Miss
Jekyll became fascinated by the new art of photography, feeling
that it was an honest form of representation, showing what was
there, unlike painting which was open to interpretation.
Writing also grew in importance to Miss Jekyll. Among the
books and articles she wrote, she contributed irregularly to the
(Manchester) *Guardian*, giving advice to amateur gardeners. In
1898, these notes were collected together and published as *Wood
and Garden: Notes and Thoughts, Practical and Critical, of a
Working Amateur; with 71 Illustrations from Photographs by the
Author*.

Harry, of course, would not read Miss Jekyll's writings. They
were for the owners of "real gardens". As a member of the
working class, he perused the *News of the World*, shocked by
police descriptions of brothels, brazen streetwalkers, and the
indiscretions of vicars. Following Sunday's dinner, he consumed
the newspaper. As he dozed "off for forty winks", Harry buried
the paper under a pile of cushions, thinking it was hidden away
from the sensibilities of the female members of his household.
As soon as Harry began to snore, Hannah folded her arms,
pretending not to see her daughters pulling out the paper and
ignoring their squeals: "Oh Ma, what a wicked world!"

A book Harry certainly did not read was *Alice in Wonderland*,
but Ada, as a bright young woman, had. It was recommended
to her by Mrs Willett's son. The author died in Guildford, in
December 1898. He was spending Christmas with his sisters at
"Chestnuts". Children were comfortable with him, grown-ups,
rarely. Only the artist Sir John Tenniel could cope with his

temperament enough to illustrate his books. Dodgson told one of his small girl admirers, "I don't think I've done more than sixty pages in eighteen weeks. I write a bit in one part of the book, then a bit in another part, and so on, all consecutively, and send it off to the printers to be set up in slip and arranged thereafter." Unlike Queen Victoria, Ada did not try to read all of the author's works. She learned from Mr Willett that Rev'd Dodgson had only written two works of fiction, *Alice in Wonderland* and *Alice through the Looking-Glass*. "The rest of his writing consists of works of mathematics. Mr Carroll is in fact a high-powered Oxford don."

Agricultural labouring continued to be the main source of income for most of Harry's class, but new developments brought new opportunities, especially for the young. Harry had always lived amongst farming folk, but his sons knew of another world, a more commercial one, which was approaching fast. One day, Percy read an advertisement, *an apprentice wanted by Guildford ironmonger Filmer & Mason*. John Dennis, a Devon farmer's son, also read it. His application was successful, and he joined the firm. In his spare time, he made bicycles. In 1895, he sold "his business" for a profit of eighty-two guineas. With the money, he opened a little bicycle shop at 94 Guildford High Street, calling it The Universal Athletic Stores. His brother Raymond joined him. Together they produced Speed King and Speed Queen bicycles, and became fascinated by motorised vehicles. In 1898, John terrified Guildfordians by driving a De Dion motorised tricycle up the High Street at the "furious speed of 16 mph". He was fined £1.

A year later, the Dennis brothers exhibited a motor vehicle at the National Cycle Show. They never tried to sell it commercially. By 1900, John and Raymond decided they were financially secure enough to own their own factory, and built the Rodboro Building in the centre of Guildford. It soon became the largest employer in town, and its goods were exported around the world.

Another new business brought a different kind of employ-ment to local workers. On 24th November 1896, the local press announced *that the well-known extensive printing works belonging to Messrs Unwin Brokers at Chilworth has burned down, including the contents of the crypt. Damage is estimated to be some £50,000.* The headquarters of the company were situated at The Gresham Press, Ludgate Hill, London. Subsequently, the company moved the factory to Broadmead, the site of an old paper mill on the River Wey. Here, they found that Broadmead was divided into plots and managed in the style of the medieval strip system, with no hedges dividing the strips. Under the Broadmead regulations, owners were entitled to turn out "one horse, mare or gelding, two cows or beasts of that kind, or five sheep for every acre" they used. Many of their workers walked in daily from Chilworth or Guildford. In time, they were joined by local men grateful for a new type of occupation beside that of agricultural labourer. Send still remained mainly agricul-tural. Later, Unwins built Gresham Gardens, in Send Road, to house Unwin workers.

However, market gardening was to become one of Send's chief occupations. In the 1890s, gravel and sand pits began to be dug in Send. Probably the first person to act as a commer-cial extractor was the nursery gardener Stephen Spooner. His men dug, by hand, in the area between Wharf Lane, Send Road, and the canal. Each shovelful was graded for size by throwing it against a mesh screen. Mr Spooner then reclaimed the land with topsoil and sludge. Later on, he began excava-tions between Send Road and Potters Lane, where once he had grown rhubarb.

Soon Mr Spooner started to plant fruit and vegetables. The produce would be sold in his sons' shops in Woking and Guildford. Samuel Boorman of Heath Farm cultivated land from the canal up to the Portsmouth Road, a distance of over a mile. He supplied Crosse & Blackwell with peas, raspberries, and other produce, which was loaded at Clandon station. Local labour was supplemented by gypsies camping in the summer. Some of their children even attended the local school.

Every Easter Sunday saw Harry and Hannah rising early. Six o'clock found them in the ruins of Newark Priory. They told the tale of how, as the mists crept up from the water meadows, they saw a shadowy figure watching, silently waiting. The winds carried the old chant *lux intrat, albescit polus, Christus venit* (a light enters, the sky grows pale, Christ comes), but the vicar was praying, "We humbly beseech, that, as by thy special grace preventing us thou dost put into our minds good desires . . . ." In the village, the children sang "the monks of the Wey seldom sang any psalms, and little they thought of religion qualms, and they could not swim, so far were they . . . those oily amorous monks of the Wey." Harry would tell of how, long ago, on another Easter morning, old King Harry's men came a-galloping. The monks fled in terror, slipped into the river, and all drowned except one. It is he who stands, watching, waiting, everlastingly waiting.

At the end of the 19th century, times were changing even faster than they had in the 16th century. Returning home, the couple walked past Newark Mill. Early in 1891, a for-sale notice announced that Newark Flour Mill would be sold by auction on 8th May 1891. Due to technological changes, the use of water-driven mills to regulate water as a source of power was declining, but they had once done so effectively. The notice stated that *the Mill is fitted with capital modern machinery, capable of turning out six hundred sacks of flour per week. The mill is in a good corn-growing district, within distance of the county and market town of Guildford, Surrey. The railway communication is of the best kind: Byfleet and Clandon stations and the South-Western railway being only a short distance on an easy road from the property. The purchaser will become entitled to £17 15s 6d per annum arising out and payable from the River Wey Navigation being the apportioned part of £52 10s per annum due to the owners of Newark, Woking and Stoke Mills and to six twenty-first parts of a toll of 10s 6d for all*

barges carrying freight and twenty loads upwards loaded above
Woodbridge, Guildford and passing down the river past Stoke Mills.
The two items here mentioned usually produce from £25 to £30 per
annum.

On 19th May 1898, Lord Lovelace's land agent informed
Harry that the "Grand Old Man" had died. Once again, he tolled
the bell. This time, it was to let Ripley know of the death of
Britain's greatest Prime Minister, William Ewart Gladstone.
He had, to Harry, seemed to have been in Parliament forever.
He knew that even before the Queen came to the throne, the
great man, with his father, had visited the "terrible Duke of
Newcastle" at Claremont, and even though he visited Lord
Rendel and held Cabinet meetings locally, Harry saw him only
once.

On the morning of Saturday, 28th May, Harry and Percy
caught the first train to Waterloo and walked across
Westminster Bridge to the Abbey. Harry would have "none of
the Underground". He told Percy, "Mr Gladstone may wish to
travel along the District line to his last resting place, but he was
a shareholder. I prefer we travel above ground, on our own two
feet." Two days previously, a train drawn by an engine called
"Gladstone" brought the statesman's body from his home,
Hawarden Castle, North Wales, to lie in state in the Great Hall
of Westminster. From 6 a.m. to 8 p.m., a quarter-of-a-million
people filed past the coffin. It was the first time a commoner had
been granted such a privilege.

Harry and Percy pushed their way along pavements packed
tight with people – some said 100,000 crowded round the
Abbey. Soldiers and policemen were everywhere, but the crowd
remained eerily silent, except for a soldier or policeman
suddenly barking orders. The crowds knew that, for a
commoner, a national funeral was a rare event. Previously,
Parliament had only paid for Nelson, Wellington, and
Palmerston. It was striking that at this funeral, civic, non-mili-
tary, and religious values were emphasized. There were no

soldiers and no uniforms, except those of the Heralds, the Speaker, the Lord Chancellor, and the dress of the Guard of Honour. Eton College was represented. Gladstone had been a scholar there.

Harry caught a glimpse of Baron Rendel of Hatchlands. "He's one of the pall-bearers," said Percy, "and they say the Duke of York and the Prince of Wales are, too." The two men saw Mrs Gladstone entering the Abbey. "She was a beauty in her youth," said Percy.

"She still is," answered Harry.

Most of Guildford mourned Mr Gladstone. They had reason to be grateful to him, as he had donated to the Guildford Institute. In spring 1893, members of the Guildford Working Men's Institute decided to form the Natural History and Microscopic Society. In 1834, it had become the Guildford Mechanics' Institute, and a year later, it coexisted with the breakaway group the Literary and Scientific Institution for Mechanics and others until 1843, when the two bodies merged to become the Guildford Institute.

From 1856, it coexisted with the Guildford Working Men's Institution until 1892, when they merged and became the Guildford and Working Men's Institution. The Institute built their own premises in 1892, in the open space next to the Royal Temperance Hotel. It was in the same style as the hotel erected in 1880 by Rev'd Francis Paynter of Stoke. On Gladstone's death, the Society consisted of ninety-eight members. They solemnly framed an autographed postcard which they had received from him, and presented it to the Institute. Normally, Gladstone never allowed his name to be used, but he had made an exception in the case of the Society. In fact, they had received the ultimate accolade: a cartoon appeared in *Punch* magazine showing Gladstone examining the Liberal majority through a microscope, together with the information that Mr Gladstone had become an honorary member of the Guildford Microscopic Natural History Society.

There were people who lived in southwest Surrey who Harry knew by name only, but who influenced his life. In March 1894, Gladstone's friend Stuart Rendel retired from the House of Commons. He became especially close to the statesman during his final premiership, when there was much parliamentary activity concerning Wales. He was consequently nicknamed the "member for Wales". It was, therefore, a surprise when he bought Hatchlands Park, close to Guildford, in 1888. The Onslows were near neighbours. An industrialist, Rendel had been called to the Bar in 1861. He subsequently became Vice-Chair of the Armstrong Gunnery Company. Acting mainly as his own architect, he improved Hatchlands and commissioned Miss Jekyll to redesign the gardens. He was raised to the peerage in 1894, and became Baron Rendel of Hatchlands in the county of Surrey. His second daughter Maud, after a protracted courtship, married Gladstone's son, the businessman Henry Neville. When visitors enter the inner hall of Hatchlands, they come face to face with the bust of Gladstone.

George Frederick Watts painted a portrait of the young Gladstone. The politician became such an admirer of the artist that he twice offered him a baronetcy, and both times the offer was declined. Watts was born on Handel's birthday in 1817. He was named after him and was inspired by the life of the musician. At the age of sixty-nine, Watts married a thirty-six-year-old designer and potter, Mary Fraser Tyler. The couple came to live in Limnerslease, a house in the village of Compton, Surrey. He said *we are two artists who are just of the same mind concerning their ideas of art*. At Compton, Watts built a studio and a gallery for his paintings. His wife designed the mortuary chapel, paid for by Watts. The chapel was built between 1896 and 1898. Aldous Huxley and other members of the Huxley family lie buried within the chapel grounds. A few years before Harry was born, slavery was abolished. He probably saw fewer than a dozen black people in his lifetime, and would have been amazed to learn that, in the next century, a twenty-nine-year-old black, American law student would be so inspired by Watts' painting of *Hope* that Barack Obama would become the 44ᵗʰ President of the United States.

In 1880, a man who was called "everybody's friend" took the tenancy of Wanborough Manor on the Hog's Back. He was The Rt. Hon. Sir Algernon West, GCB, Principal Private Secretary to Mr Gladstone, and entertained the great and the good in the Elizabethan manor. Visitors included Otto von Bismark, the "Iron Chancellor" of Germany, Queen Victoria, who planted a tree in the grounds, and Prime Minister Gladstone. The Prime Minister often stayed at Wanborough, and held Cabinet meetings in the manor. In 1920, Sir Algernon wrote a book, *Contemporary Life: On Men of My Day in Public Life*. It was Sir Algernon who said of Gladstone, "after years of intimacy, private and official, I have never felt capable of adequately depicting a hundredth part of his complex character." Sir Algernon retired when Mr Gladstone left office in 1894.

Sir Algernon had been one of Surrey's most distinguished residents. He had been a member of Parliament, Justice of the Peace, Chairman of the Board of the Inland Revenue, a Privy Counsellor, and in June 1902, was invested with the Knight Grand Cross, Order of the Bath (GCB). Sir Algernon was also a director of the South Eastern Railway and, in 1891, was instrumental in Wanborough station being opened. Harry may have been surprised to learn that Sir Algernon considered travelling by rail to a station would be more comfortable for his distinguished guests than negotiating the steep hill of the Hog's Back from Guildford by coach and horses. However, he never liked steam: "You cannot talk to it like you can a horse." A man who throughout Queen Victoria's reign had been at the centre of things, in 1908, in his *Recollections*, said *we are getting better, probably in many things, though with no alarming rapidity, but certainly in a broader and kindlier tone in public life*. . . . He may have forgotten Mr Gladstone's warning of *this dreadful military spirit*. . . .

Eighteen ninety-nine saw the start of the Second Boer War. The first men to enlist were reservists, and this must have caused considerable hardship because, on 7th November 1899, an entry in the school logbook records "Collection made amongst children towards the Fund for the relief of the families of the Reservists." The 2nd Battalion of the Queen's Royal West Surrey Regiment served in the Boer War, and a total of forty-four officers served either with the battalion or on staff duties with the Army.

Miss Prue, who lived in the big house on the road to Cobham, was one of Harry's favourite people. One day, he found her sitting alone in the church. He knew that her father, General Sir Arthur Graham, was to be buried the next day. Harry saw the young girl was clutching a small box. "I hear on the grapevine Master Eric has been around."

"Yes, he came to say goodbye to father, but he had already died."

When he was a young man, the General had "got a maid into trouble". He had behaved well, keeping the child with the mother and educating him privately. However, Eric turned out to be a wild boy, something of a conman. Often, the police were heard banging on the General's door. He denied that his son was in the house even though he knew the boy was hiding in the attic. Eric joined the Navy, disliked it, and joined the Army, and when bored, changed regiments, not bothering to tell the authorities. He had done time, and loved nobody but Prue, whom he called "Childee". Harry took the box from the girl's hand, and opened it. He found a small bronze Maltese cross, with a crown mounted by a lion, inscribed *For Valour*. For the first and only time in his life, he held the Victoria Cross. "It's Eric's," explained Prue. "He wanted it buried with father."

"It will be done, Miss Prue," replied Harry.

In 1887, the formidable Mrs Dibble of the Anchor Inn died, followed by lovely Annie in 1895, and a year later, the other daughter, Harriet. Alf Dibble, the son, immediately sold the Anchor to Mr and Mrs Gibbons, Guildford hoteliers. At the end of the 1890s, the stock market crashed, business withered away, and even the Ripley cycle trade declined. However, people remembered how, on one Sunday in 1894, the police in Kingston-upon-Thames reckoned twenty thousand cyclists passed through the town en route to Ripley. The Dibbles used to sell as many as 400 meals at any one time. Even fictional characters like E. W. Hornung's *Raffles* rode along the "incomparable Ripley Road". A man who arrived at the Anchor out of hours was told by Annie, "We can serve you with cold ham, cold mutton, or cold beef."

"Anything hot?" he enquired.

"Mustard," came the reply.

However, the cyclists still collected and organised the Road Menders' Feeds, hot suppers for the old men who worked on the road between the Angel at Thames Ditton and the Anchor. The dinners were held from 1890 to 1908, with the road menders entertained, "plied with a packet of 'baccy', and each one given half a pound of tea for the Misses".

By 1898, the fame of Lord Lovelace's Hautboy had grown. A viscount's wife, Lady Harberton, stopped to take midday lunch in the coffee room. Mrs Martha Sprague, the hotel's landlady, refused admittance "as the lady was clad from the crown of her head to the soles of her feet in so-called rational dress (baggy knickerbockers)." She directed Lady Harberton to a room off the public bar, where she found the smoke-filled room and the company of workmen abominable. She insisted on returning to the coffee room. Mrs Sprague replied sharply, "Not in those clothes." A court case followed. Mrs Sprague insisted "it would be fatal to my business were I to admit women who plied the Portsmouth Road in their 'skin-tights'." The all-male jury agreed with Mrs Sprague. However, Lord Coleridge, Lady Harberton's lawyer, predicted that Mrs Sprague's attitude would soon be seen as "purblind and perverted".

The 20th century dawned, bringing with it undreamed-of challenges and opportunities. Ockham strongly felt these changes. There was a new Earl of Lovelace, a new rector of Ockham, and a largely-new population. The parish needed to be, and was, reorganized. Surrey children still went a-Maying, dressing up and going round to the big houses with baskets of flowers or a miniature maypole decorated with hawthorn bunches, chanting "the first of May, give us a penny and we'll run away."

On Ripley Green, the village children weaved in and out around the maypole. However, Mayday festivities were often bawdy. Harry remembered that the young chimney sweeps behaved especially badly. In 1875, when it became illegal to employ them, the more sedate Morris dancers took over. "Jack in the Green" was still lauded on many a Mayday. Laurels were woven into a frame made of green garden netting; sometimes sprigs of blossom were added. It hung from the Jack's shoulders by straps, with a hole for him to peer through. In Guildford, he was known as the "Guildford bush".

It was a short journey from Ripley along the Portsmouth Road to Downside-cum-Cobham. In the tiny hamlet, mothers presented their eldest daughters with a bunch of flowers placed on top of a stick. "Here is a present for the Queen of the May. May the Maypole dance bring you a good husband!" In another village, the author recalls in *Some Reminiscences of Old Byfleet*, *schools were closed for the 1st May. The children used to assemble in some central spot dressed in their very best, each child carrying a large or small bunch of flowers more or less tastefully arranged, fixed to the end of a pole four to six feet long, which they carried in procession. Some of these Maypoles were very nicely got up. The procession was arranged with the biggest children in front tailing down to the little ones at the rear. They called at the houses of the better class and halting in order chanted the old rhyme:*

The first of May's garland day,
Please to remember the Maypole;
We don't come here but once a year,
So please to remember the Maypole!
Ladies and gentleman would make a point of coming out and go up
and down the line inspecting the maypole, giving such praise and encour-
agement as they felt was due. . . .

As with the old May Day customs, the past did not
completely vanish. In Miss Jekyll's "Lovely Old Guildford", the
Old Bank in the High Street (established 1765) was altered and
extended in 1899. The front was retained *at the special request of*
HRH Princess Louise, Marchioness of Lorne, and the Rt. Hon. the
Viscount Midleton, Lord Lieutenant of Surrey, on behalf of The Old
Guildford Society (founded 1896).

At the end of the century, many parents were annoyed to
learn that the school leaving age was to be raised to twelve. The
new century would bring Harry much sadness. Hannah
continued to delight in the pale mauve foxgloves growing round
the "back door". When he reached seventy years of age, Harry
proudly declined to receive 5/- a week, free.

CHAPTER SIX

1900–1914

Edwardian Summers but Winter Approaches

The 1901 census shows Henry is now sixty-one. He is still an agricultural labourer, but does not say who his employer is. Hannah is sixty-three. All her babies have gone, and she misses having a toddler around the house. They are living in the centre of Ripley, in Rose Lane. It leads directly off the High Street going towards Ockham, and is opposite the Green. Ryde House School is in Rose Lane, and Harry's grandson Charlie remembered Mr Pierce, the headmaster, calling on the old man in his nineties. The school had suffered a fire, and most of the records were lost. Harry remembered almost every detail. He told Mr Pierce how much he regretted the school's sanatorium being housed in gracious Yew Tree House at the end of the High Street. Often, as Harry walked along Rose Lane, he passed Cobham Cottages and wondered why the churchwardens of St Andrew's parish church bought them in the 17th century as alms houses for Cobham's poor. They seem as if they belong to the 18th century, but the timber frames show they are much older. Harry felt "the old folk must have felt uncomfortable ending their days in Ripley, such a different village from Cobham."

At the time of the census, Harry is no longer sexton to Ripley parish church. There is an entry in the church accounts of "Worsfold paid £19 13 4d for the period from Easter 1897 to 1898, for duties as sexton and acting as clerk." However, by

1892, the name of Mr Daws begins to appear. In 1904, he is acting sexton, and by 1907, Mr Daws is referred to as sexton and clerk, and no mention is made of Alice Daws, who boarded for a while with Harry and Hannah. The full records of the time have been lost. Harry remained proud that "my Hannah was held in such high esteem that when her glass eye fell out at morning prayer and rolled down the church aisle, the congregation gathered together and purchased a new one for her. You could not tell the difference between that and her good eye. It looked exactly the same."

Now only two sons remained with the couple. Arthur, sixteen, a baker's assistant and bread man, possibly worked in the baker's in the High Street on the corner of Rose Lane. The villagers used the shopkeeper as an alarm clock. At 4 a.m. every morning, the baker noisily opened the shop and started baking. At one time, there were at least three bread shops in Ripley. The other son, Edmund, seventeen, was a groom on a local stud farm. He would take the horses for shoeing to the local blacksmith, probably using the forge at the corner of Rose Lane. The place was always busy, and there was always a queue as the blacksmith was also a wheelwright and farrier. He repaired many things, such as agricultural machinery, kitchen ranges, boys' hoops, penny farthings, and the new bicycle. This was a man who knew how to handle horses as well as treat their diseases and injuries. He would be on first-name terms with the local carters, such as "newcomer" Charles Hilderley. A "roaming-man", he had lived all over Berkshire, and by 1900, had brought George and the rest of the family to live at Wisley Common, close to wealthy relatives.

Horses were prized possessions. They were regarded as almost equal to human beings. Therefore, farmers demanded they were well looked after. Much time was spent grooming them because a good farm horse, like a Clydesdale, could perform numerous tasks – in fact, no other source of locomotion or power could compare.

A good carter knew as much about his horses as any vet or blacksmith, and understood why horses' tails should not be docked. They needed length to flick the flies away, but the danger was they could get caught in the cart. Charles Hilderley stated, "a horse is fine, but a mare is like a woman: once she takes against you, she'll start a' kicking, 'tis very seldom you can do much with her after that."

He told the story of an old doctor who thrashed his mare over her ears with his stick. "Be careful Doctor," he warned. "She'll throw you off and roll you into a ditch and leave you there" – which is precisely what she did. One night, coming home after midnight, the mare wandered in to the stable yard, alone. There was no sign of the doctor. Next morning, they found him, dead in a ditch. He had died from fright and cold.

By Harry's time, oxen were rarely used on farms. Any blacksmith will tell you that shoeing an ox is more difficult than shoeing a horse. They have far less nail than a horse's hoof, and can be easily injured or permanently lamed. All sorts of horses worked on farms – geldings, cobs, mares, draught horses – but it was the stud stallions that blacksmiths feared the most. Grooms walked them around the countryside to serve broodmares. Harry remembered them coming through Ripley, great-shouldered animals, highly-strung, heads tossing, snorting, arching necks, nostrils distended, ears laying flat back, and eyes showing white, led by a lone man just by a halter. The horse would catch the eye of any young filly, and the dandy little man had a way with him too. Every pretty girl in the village noted the stud groom.

Hannah, like most mothers, kept a sharp eye on her daughters. Nevertheless, the groom usually left a "bun or two in the oven" behind him. When the stallion came into the smithy for shoeing, the blacksmith went carefully. He would hope the animal would quickly settle down, as he was in danger of being kicked in the face. Often, the beast was a full eighteen-and-a-half hands high, and more than a ton in weight. If he reared up and stayed frisky, the smithy door would be bolted, the shutters closed, and candles or oil lamps lit. The blacksmith would take a draft of beer, telling the lad, "give me a can of water," and then he threw it with all his might over the horse, drenching the creature. Immediately, he picked up a huge anvil and brought it down with a bang. When the horse stood quite still, trembling, it was then – and only then –that the blacksmith shoed him. Villagers said, "he uses a secret language to speak to it, learned from a tinker." Even witchcraft was hinted at.

Ripley said "'Old Molly' it was who puts the evil eye on the animal." Like all villages, Ripley had its ancient woman wise in the ways of witchcraft, who knew all manner of spells. Did she not visit a family in Wisley? The sons were going into Ripley, and the old woman asked them for a lift to her cottage. They refused. Travelling along Wisley Lane, going towards the Portsmouth Road, they threw a stone at a hare, hitting its back right leg. When the boys arrived at Ripley, "Old Molly" was sitting in her cottage by the fire, her right leg bound up. She gave them such a look. . . .

There was not a farm or a cottage where "old Molly" could not get a bag of "taties", a bit of butter, or a jug of milk. A farmer, a newcomer to Ripley, ordered her off his land. The next night, she could be seen standing in his fields, alone in the moonlight, chanting. A few days later, thistles appeared, ruining the farmer's crop.

Harry had no fear of "old Molly". He remembered a night under a harvest moon with a gypsy girl. In old age, he boasted that he never took so much as an aspirin, but he did not tell that he knew an old woman who could bury a potato to ward off warts, or give a mixture to cure the cramps, or cast a spell . . . .

In many ways, cut off from the main world, Ripley remained part of the old world and was fearful when, on 22nd January 1901, Queen Victoria died. Edward VII came to the throne, a man Harry did not approve of. He did not "hold with the Head of the Church of England being a serial adulterer". There is no mention of Her Majesty's death in the Ripley School logbook, nor is there a record of the children being given time off for her funeral. Six months before, on 12th June 1900, the Rev'd Tuke presented the school with a portrait of the Queen-Empress. No reason is given for the gift.

As the 20th century approached, a new headmaster, Harry Tilbury, took over from the former teachers Mr and Mrs Ward. On 2nd June 1902, an entry in red ink appears in the logbook: PEACE IS PROCLAIMED. Finally, the long years of the Boer War had come to an end. On 6th June, the school celebrated the British victory. In the school lists of 1905, the name Alice Perrin appears. The little girl's full name was Alice Ethel Ladysmith Perrin. She was born in 1900. In February of that year, following four months of being besieged, Ladysmith, in Natal, was relieved. However, it was not an aristocrat who spoke to the crowds from the steps of Holy Trinity, but the Mayor, Henry Peak.

Mafeking, in Cape Province, had also withstood a siege that had lasted for seven months. In May 1900, it too was relieved, and on 21st May, the schoolchildren enjoyed a national holiday. In Guildford, flags flew wildly, and during the evening, crowds thronged into the High Street and joined in with the choirs of Holy Trinity and St Mary's, singing patriotic songs. Once again, it was Mayor Peak who addressed the people "from the steps of the 'Upper' church".

On 20th June 1902, Edward VII was crowned. The schoolchildren enjoyed a national holiday. It was also the year the Education Act brought about Local Education Authorities (LEAs), and board schools became known as council schools. However, the cost of maintaining the buildings remained in the hands of local supporters. Another effect of the Act was that "children no longer taught children." Pupil teachers were not allowed to teach in schools until they were sixteen years old. Formerly, they had been apprenticed to a school at thirteen and "learned on the job". Once a week, the young person attended a pupil–teacher centre. From then on, local authorities gave bursaries to secondary schools. This enabled promising children to become "special pupils" and train as pupil teachers. However, the authorities continued to maintain strict control:

The report and accounts of Ripley National School state:

Report of the Religious Instruction by the Diocesan Inspector, 23rd January, 1902. Mixed school: The work has suffered considerably owing to sickness among the children, and several changes in the staff. . . .The Upper Class showed much interest in its work, and is being well taught on the right lines. The Middle Division was somewhat weak. Standards 1 & 2 showed a creditable knowledge of Bible History.

Infant schools . . . In both of them the children were bright, interested, and well informed, answering readily and accurately. The results reflect credit on the teachers.

A.B. MILNER, DIOCESAN INSPECTOR.

The Balance Sheet shows teachers' salaries amounted to: £330 6s 8d per year.
The headmaster and wife's received a combined salary of: £150 0s 0d per year.
The Infant Mistress received, £65 per annum and the Assistant Mistress, received, £35 per year.
The pupil-teacher received, £10 per year
The caretaker received, £20 per year.
Monitors were given 1s 6d per week.

Additionally, following complaints about the school's facilities, flush toilets replaced buckets. In Ripley, evening classes for adults began even though the movement had started in the late 18th century. The authorities in Ripley gave good reports and praise *for those who after a hard day's work on the farm, are prepared to give up their free evenings to study to improve their skills and knowledge.*

The first Empire Day took place a year after the Queen's death, on her birthday – 24th May 1902. Although it was not an official holiday, many schools celebrated the day, including Ripley School: "The idea of the day was to remind children that they formed part of the British Empire, and that they might think with others in lands across the sea, what it meant to be sons and daughters of such a glorious Empire."

On 22nd January 1908, Thomas Marriot Berridge, former head teacher and a school manager, presented a Union Jack to the school. He wished to draw the pupils' attention to the "Empire on which the sun never set". Lady Lovelace offered a tree from her estate which the school could make into a flagstaff. This was erected by the school entrance. The children had the Union Jack explained to them, and a public ceremony was held of "hoisting the flag". In future, saluting the flag became part of Empire Day ceremonies, accompanied by the children singing *Jerusalem* or *God Save the King*.

An ardent imperialist, the 12th Earl of Meath, Reginald Brabazon, was a keen promoter of the Empire movement and Empire Day. He said "it reminded children of the watch-words of the British Empire: Responsibility, Sympathy, Duty and Self-Sacrifice." The Earl was related to Miss Jekyll's close friend, the watercolour artist Hercule Brabazon. The Earl and his wife devoted much of their time to the consideration of social problems and the relief of human suffering. From 1882 to 1883, they leased Ottershaw Park.

In 1908, diphtheria swept across the country, and Ripley also suffered. Prior to immunisation in the 1920s, the disease was a major cause of death in children. Schoolmaster Best recorded that two village children, Doris Peters and Hilda Barratt, had died in the Woodbridge Isolation Hospital. Hilda had been a prizewinner for two years for good attendance at the school. Later in the year, another child died – Bessie Fuller. She had contracted the disease from her sister. Ripley people muttered amongst themselves that patients were being sent home too early and spreading the infection. Hannah and Harry feared for their own children.

A year later, Mr and Mrs Best left Ripley School to take charge of another school. The managers presented the couple with a silver teapot and a tea service. The staff and children gave them a clock. A young, newly-married couple, Mr and Mrs George Hilderley received a slate clock, but this was presented to them by the RHS committee of Wisley Gardens.

Following Mr Wilson's death in 1902, Quaker businessman Sir Thomas Hanbury paid £5,000 for Oakwood and presented the garden, described as "a place to make difficult plants grow successfully", to the RHS. With the sixty acres of Oakwood came the adjoining Glebe Farm. Sir Thomas also acquired Weatherhill, Mr Wilson's gardener's cottage, a small farmhouse, thatched fruit room, barn, and a few sheds. However, he would be more famous as the owner of La Mortola, the gardens he created on the Italian Riviera, where he died in 1907. However, Sir Thomas knew Surrey well. He was born in the upper-class village of Clapham, and was friendly with Miss Jekyll and photographer Francis Frith, who photographed so much of Surrey.

For some time, the RHS had wanted to leave Chiswick and were actively looking for a new site "beyond the radius of London smog". Some members complained that Wisley was an unsuitable spot. It was out of the way and the soil was poor. Nevertheless, the Superintendent of Chiswick moved to Wisley in the spring of 1904, and by the following May, the move was completed. During the first full year of RHS membership, more than 6,000 people visited Wisley, and a wide drive from the entrance to Weatherhill was constructed.

In 1907, a course was started "for young men not exceeding the age of 22 to study practical gardening and laboratory work for two years". At the end of this time, if their work was up to standard, they would receive the Wisley Diploma in Practical Horticulture (WDPH).

In 1896, George (a son of Charles Hilderley) joined Oakwood. He was born far away in Farncombe, Berkshire. His family roamed around so much that "I hope I will never leave Wisley." George, "being an honest sober and industrious young man", became a particular favourite of Mr Wilson's. He grew into a much-loved figure, respected by the RHS and remembered with great affection by horticulturalists and students everywhere.

George came from a family of twelve. He began working at eleven years of age, labouring for Mr Giles of Pond Farm, and later for Mr Gaylord of Deer Farm. Here, he received 4/- a day. Later, he joined the outdoor staff of Mr E. M. Buxton at Foxwarren Park, as a gardening lad, receiving 6/- for a twelve-hour day. On 2nd June 1900, the Head Gardener, Mr James R. Hall, wrote to Mr Alfred Tatvall, Head Gardener of Oakwood Gardens: *It gives me much pleasure to certify that G. Hilderley has been here, as lad, in the gardens for 4 years during which time I have always found him a very painstaking, civil, obliging, and steady lad. And his all round experience here 'inside and out' should make him very useful, anywhere.*

On 10th October 1903, Mr Tatvall recommended George to the RHS: *He has a very good knowledge of flower and kitchen garden work. Thoroughly understands growing cucumbers, tomatoes and all manner of ground work. He is a young man that I can with confidence thoroughly recommend.*

A true Edwardian, George expected plants to grow in orderly patterns, and ladies to hide from the sun under parasols. He was shocked when Miss Jekyll appeared on Wisley's Battleston Hill armed with a spade and voicing opinions: "as for those boots . . . !"

At the turn of the century, Miss Jekyll was approaching sixty, and famous. She was writing at least one book a year; altogether she wrote fifteen. In 1904, Miss Jekyll published her masterpiece, *Old West Surrey*, and wrote in the preface that *so many and so great have been the changes within the last half century that I have*

thought desirable to note, while it may still be done, what I can remember
of the ways and lives of the habitations of the older people of the working
class of the country I have lived in continuously since I was a very young
child.

So many people wished to visit her at Munstead Wood that she was forced to write *I must ask my kind readers not to take it amiss if I mention here that I cannot undertake to show* [the garden] *on the spot. I am a solitary worker; I am growing old and tired.* Even as she aged, Miss Jekyll preferred designing big gardens – they paid better, and she was always hard up.

In 1904, she discovered, in Snowdenham Lane, Bramley, several small cottages which were about to be pulled down, leaving some unused land. It overlooked Miss Jekyll's old home and was within sound of the working mill which she loved so much. She bought the land and persuaded Lutyens to build Millmead House, a small country house, in the arts-and-crafts style. It is still considered to be one of the prettiest in the neighbourhood. Of course, Miss Jekyll designed the garden. She always said how difficult it was to create what was in the mind's eye: "I come round the corner suddenly of the house and garden; I catch it unaware. It seems to me all right; and then I enjoy it – I enjoy it very much . . . ."

Millmead House gave Miss Jekyll an additional income, and maintained her relationship with Bramley. Until the day she died, she wrote for the parish magazine and continued to be fascinated by the old, dying crafts: *Cider is still made with the old wooden press. The apples are first pressed by a cooler in the cider mill. Heaps of apples . . . many are muddy and bruised but in they go mud and all.*

Sir Thomas had another woman friend, younger than Miss Jekyll. This was Ellen Willmott, born in 1858. Miss Jekyll described her as "the greatest, living woman gardener". In her twenties, she received a substantial inheritance from her godmother, Helen Tasker. This enabled Miss Willmott to buy Le Chateau de Tressetu, near Aix-les-Bains, France, in 1890. On her father's death in 1892, Ellen inherited the family estates at Warley, Brentwood, Essex, "a place free from the foul fogs and smoke of London," and on the death of her mother, she received a further legacy.

Ellen Wilmott was pretty, intelligent, dressed fashionably, and totally uneducated. Nobody controlled or advised her. Ellen became obsessed: "my plants and gardens come before anything else in my life." Out of control, she developed a passion for collecting and cultivating plants, and was always hoping to discover new species. In order to do this, she sponsored expeditions to the Middle East and China.

It is said that during her lifetime, Miss Willmott cultivated more than 100,000 species, even introducing some to Kew. She employed over a hundred gardeners, sacking any who allowed a weed to grow amongst the flowers, and employed only men – "women would be a disaster in the border."

Ellen Willmott bought another garden in Ventimiglia, northern Italy, and developed a close friendship with her neighbour, Sir Thomas Hanbury. He was the man who purchased Oakwood and donated it to the RHS. Ellen was already a member of the Society. She joined it in 1894, and was appointed a trustee in 1903. She received many accolades from the horticultural world. Along with Miss Jekyll, Ellen Willmott was one of the few women to receive the Victoria Medal. In 1905, she was among the first women to be elected a fellow of the Linnean Society of London.

In 1912, she received the Grande Médaille Geoffroy St Hilaire from the *Société nationale d'acclimatation de France*, and the Dean Hole medal from the National Rose Society in 1914. Numerous people paid a visit to her gardens at Warley, including their majesties Queen Mary, Queen Alexandra, and Princess Victoria.

Seventeen years younger than Miss Jekyll, she formed a friendship with the older woman. Ellen stayed with her at Munstead Wood, writing notes from there on its headed paper.

However, unlike Miss Jekyll, she was not a business woman, artist, or garden designer, but like Miss Jekyll, she did write books. They included *Warley in Spring and Summer* and *Genus Rosa*. The two unmarried ladies shared another passion – both of them were keen photographers.

As Ellen aged, her eccentricities increased. Sadly, Viscountess Wolsey's daughter's suggestion was not acted upon. In March 1898, a luncheon took place hosted by the Viscountess. Her daughter suggested that two of the guests, fifty-five-year-old William Robinson and forty-four-year-old Miss Willmott, should marry each other as both were keen gardeners and both very rich. If they had, perhaps Miss Willmott would not have taken to carrying a revolver in her handbag, booby-trapping her gardens, and being arrested on suspicion of shoplifting.

Gradually, Ellen lost her gardens. They were sold to pay her debts. In her seventy-seventh year, Ellen Wilmott died, alone, penniless, and a forgotten figure, except that she had continued to visit gardens, scattering seeds of the sea horse into flower borders. As dusk falls, they appear silvery-white, spectre-like. Gardeners mutter, one to another, "Miss Wilmott's ghost . . . ."

Gardeners were not overly concerned with foxes or lack of them, but you can hear the Surrey voice of one elderly woman, a widow of a lodging keeper, who wrote to the Surrey Union Hunt, on 27th February 1900: *I am sorry to tell you a fox killed one of my geese this morning. Bit its head off. I could not have lost it for a sovereign. As it layed and of soon sit. It is a great loss to me. Sir, Your obedient, Annie Bowring.*

Many Surrey people felt the county was becoming a play-ground to provide shooting for wealthy idlers, and certainly the elite was changing. In 1906, H. R. Taylor, author of *The Old Surrey Fox Hounds*, commented: *Unfortunately, however, foxes are not as plentiful at present in certain districts of the Surrey territory as they used to be, for the shooting interest is acquiring predominance. . . . In the northern parts of the Old Surrey country bricks and mortar*

and wire render hunting practically impossible. One may anticipate an
extension of that development; it seems to be inevitable.

However, in 1904, the Surrey Hunt acquired a new, bright young master, Mr Frederick Gordon Dalziel of Norfolk Park, Epsom Downs, a member of the Norfolk starch and mustard firm. He was one of the youngest masters in Britain and considered to be an excellent judge of a horse. He was always superbly mounted and well turned out. Mr Dalziel insisted that members of the hunt display the primrose yellow of Surrey Hunt on their collars. He offered to resign when the *Daily News* published an article, on 4th July 1906, accusing him of bad estate management, trying to dispose of a virtuous tenant, and responsible for the suicide of an itinerant worker. In October 1907, the Master's offer of resignation was rejected. During the time of Mr Dalziel's office, fifty couples of hounds were added to the Surrey Hunt pack and it hunted four days a week.

At the start of the new century, Harry realized that the aristocracy was changing. In 1906, the 2nd Earl of Lovelace, who was not a keen hunting man, died. Harry was shocked to learn His Lordship was not to be buried, but to follow the heathen practice of being cremated at Woking crematorium. However, he did follow tradition in having his ashes interned with his parents in the family mausoleum at Horsley Towers. The 2nd Earl was succeeded by his half-brother, Lionel Fortescue King, son of the 1st Earl and his second wife. He would be the last of the Lovelaces to live in Surrey.

In 1907, another death occurred in one of the great Surrey families. This was William More-Molyneux. He was succeeded by Gwendoline, the daughter of his younger brother, Admiral Sir Robert More-Molyneux. A widow with a daughter, Christobel, she married Brigadier-General Frank Longbourne. He later took the name of More-Molyneux Longbourne. As General Longbourne, he served in the First World War, was mentioned in despatches thirteen times, awarded the Distinguished Service Order (DSO), and later appointed

Commander of the Order of Saint Michael and Saint George (CMG). He returned to Loseley with four of his men, ex-soldiers. The 1,400-acre estate remained mainly agricultural, but in 1916 the famous Jersey herd was established. This formed the basis for Loseley's famous dairy products, and a less aristocratic, but more commercial approach began.

New money was coming into Surrey. The Westons had long gone from Sutton Place, leaving behind them only the blood-stained ruff of Sir Thomas More and a crystal pomegranate once belonging to Catherine of Aragon. In 1900, the newspaper tycoon Alfred Harmsworth, Lord Northcliffe, became the tenant. He was not a hunting man, and said, "the quiet I find here is the best thing money has given me."

He must have felt the need of peace. Born in Dublin in 1865, Northcliffe is still considered "one of the greatest figures ever to stride down Fleet Street". He hugely influenced British popular opinion, which one commentator described as "keen and eager. Intelligent, but also superficial and very badly educated." In 1896, Northcliffe founded the *Daily Mail*, dismissed by Prime Minister Robert Cecil, Lord Salisbury, as "written for office boys by office boys". In 1903, he bought the *Daily Mirror*. Two years later, he rescued from financial ruin *The Observer*, *The Times*, and (in 1908) *The Sunday Times*.

In 1888, Northcliffe married Mary Elizabeth Milner, who became a public figure in her own right, awarded the Dame Grand Cross of the Order of the British Empire and the Dame of Grace Order of St John. The couple had no children, but it was rumoured Northcliffe had had a son when he was seventeen by a servant of his parents, a sixteen-year-old girl. It is said he also told his men friends, in the greatest confidence, that he did have a family – two sons and a daughter – by an Irish woman whom he met in 1900.

His tenancy of Sutton Place expired in 1918, and Northcliffe left Surrey. Afterwards, his health became unpredictable, and he died in 1922, leaving three months' wages to each of his employees. A year later, on 23rd April, Viscountess Northcliffe married a friend and colleague of her husband's, widower Sir Robert Arundal Hudson, GBE. He was a prominent Liberal and the Party's treasurer. He died in 1927; Lady Hudson, in 1963.

Lord Northcliffe is recorded as saying "people are so much more interesting than things." No record exists of his comments when one of his great friends and brother of the Chief Scout, Lord Baden-Powell, fiddled around and eventually fixed up Sutton Place with a wireless telephone.

The Wisley Gardens' staff were looked after by the RHS in their old age. However, it was a constant worry for working-class people, especially if they had no children. A man who, unlike George Abbott, had not been born in Surrey, William Whiteley of the Whiteley department store, Bayswater, built the biggest collection of almshouses in the country, near Weybridge. Whiteley was born in Yorkshire in 1832, and was apprenticed at sixteen to a draper. He visited the Great Exhibition and fell in love with London. He came to live in London and worked for a City firm. He then started out on his own. In 1907, Whiteley left £1,000,000 to purchase a park and create homes for 350 of his aged employees. The residents received free medical attention and care, and no bills for electric light, gas, coal, or water. A bronze seated figure of industry displays a plaque to the founder "as an encouragement for others to do likewise". Sealed in a bottle under the memorial is a parchment plan of the village drawn up by Frank Atkinson, the architect.

The Onslows did hunt, and retained the old style of leadership. The 4th Earl of Onslow continued his political career. From 1900–3 he was Undersecretary of State for the Colonies, and from 1903–5 was President of the Board of Agriculture and a Cabinet member. In 1905, "this good straight Englishman of the best type" became a member of the Privy Council, a formal body which advises the Sovereign. Members swear "By Almighty God to be a true and faithful servant unto the King's Majesty as one of his Majesty's Privy Council."

Between 1905 and 1911, Lord Onslow was appointed as Lord Chairman of the House of Lords. However, in Hillier's late fifties, his health began to fail and he retired from public life. Steps in the grounds were covered with ramps so he could use his bath chair and continue to enjoy the gardens.

The 4th Earl of Onslow was buried on 27th October in the family vault at Merrow. He left £7,477 5s 3d. Shortly before Hillier's death, he visited his son Huia at his home in Hampstead. In June, while holidaying in the Dolomites, he dived into Lake Misurina and hit his head on a submerged rock. It left him paralysed. Eventually, Huia returned to Cambridge to continue his research into genetics. He made important discoveries in the study of dominant genes as illustrated by eye and hair colour inherited from parents.

Of course, it was the eldest son Richard, Viscount Cranley, who became the 5th Earl. He would not have the brilliance of his brother or follow in the distinguished footsteps of his father. Richard described himself as being *idle as the idlest at Oxford*. He entered the Diplomatic Service. In 1904, he went to the British Embassy in St Petersburg, where he attended a court ball for 7,000 guests in the Winter Palace. The last person Richard saw entering the room was Tsar Nicholas, who wandered from table to table making sure that everyone had what they wanted to eat and drink.

In 1906, Richard married Violet Bampfylde, daughter of the 3rd Baron Poltimore of Devon. The couple returned to St Petersburg. In 1908, they came back to England, and Onslow retired from the Foreign Office. On his father's death in 1911, Richard entered the House of Lords. In March 1913, the 5th Earl began a series of improvements to Clandon Park. These were interrupted by the onset of the Great War.

He said in old age, "my career, though laborious, has not been distinguished and my own humble achievements would hardly merit the trouble of record." However, perhaps it was Richard who gave Surrey the greatest legacy of any of the Onslows: in

1933, he donated Stag Hill to Guildford, where once the kings of England had hunted. Now there are "all manner of people" who climb to the top of the hill. Guildfordians decided to bear witness and built a great cathedral.

In 1936, Cosmo Gordon Lang, Archbishop of Canterbury, laid the foundation stone. One hundred and eighty-three architects entered the competition to design the building. It was won by Sir Edward Maufe. World War II interrupted work on the Cathedral Church of the Holy Spirit. It was not opened until many years later, by HM Queen Elizabeth II, on 17th May 1961. As you approach Guildford, the Cathedral is the first building you see on the skyline. It stands a witness to the greatness of God, and a reminder that man always overcomes evil, eventually.

Mrs Greville too was a lady who did not come from the best of society. She lived extravagantly and, unlike Miss Wilmott, died wealthy. In 1891, the Hon. Ronald Greville married Margaret Helen Anderson, the illegitimate daughter of a self-made multimillionaire brewer. She famously said, "I would rather be beeress than a peeress." In 1906, Mr and Mrs Greville descended on Surrey to live at Polesden Lacey *in the village of beeches* (Great Bookham, Dorking). The mansion nestles under the north Downs, enjoying commanding views over the Surrey hills.

As nearby Clandon had been built as "a place for entertaining", so Polesden Lacey was used to play host to flamboyant characters such as Richard Brinsley Sheridan, the 18th-century politician and playwright. He also managed Drury Lane's Theatre Royal. Sheridan was a man of great extravagance and lover of drink. In 1798, his stage manager foretold bankruptcy, commenting, "Such things as wood and canvas not to be had, yet three thousand guineas given for an estate."

In 1809, the Theatre Royal burned down. Sheridan is reported as saying, "a man may surely be allowed to take a glass of wine by his own fireside." The disaster added to his mounting financial problems and increasingly precarious health. Sheridan was forced to leave Polesden, and died in 1816.

He had said "there is no possibility of being witty without a little ill-nature." Edward VII thought Mrs Greville's gift for hospitality amounted to positive genius; on the other hand, society hostess Mrs Leslie observed, "Maggie Greville, I would rather have an open sewer in my living room."

In fact, Mrs Greville's life may have taken a more conventional course if her husband had not died of throat cancer in 1908. This left her a relatively young widow. She did not marry again. The Hon. Ronald Greville was considered by some "an awesomely dull man", but his photograph shows a suave, dandified figure clutching a cigarette in a gloved hand, observing the world through heavy-lidded eyes. Greville was a popular landlord, fond of steeplechasing, and rode many races before his premature end. *The Sunday Times* described him as *witty, good natured, typically Irish.*

By the time of her husband's death, Polesden had been converted into a house fit for royalty by Mewes and Davis, the architects of the London Ritz Hotel. Mrs Greville's abilities as a hostess, her cuisine and elaborate menus made her renowned even amongst Edwardian hostesses, who are remembered for their culinary extravagances. Margaret Greville loved company, especially royalty, saying of the deported King of Greece, "I still love him even though he is an ex-king." However, it would be the Windsors who had a special place in her heart, and she in theirs.

Mrs Greville agreed with the comment made by many: "My dears, I know I'm not an educated woman." It was uncertain how she had managed to marry so well and rise so high. At the time of her birth, her parents were not married. "Mrs Ronnie's" father was William McEwan, a near-teetotaller, self-made man, and multimillionaire brewer. He described himself as a great self-improver, studying Shakespeare in his spare time. McEwan established the Fountain Brewery, famous for its McEwan's

Export and Indian Pale Ale, a favourite with the British Army. It was said Margaret was introduced to her husband, a friend of Edward VII, because her father "got Edward VII out of a financial jam".

She was no beauty, but she was clever, and Greville managed to propel her into the centre of the Marlborough set. Eventually, Mrs Greville's parents did marry, and she never forgave Edinburgh society for the judgmental attitude it had shown to her parents. In the year of her husband's death, Mr McEwan came to live with his daughter. She doted on her father, and he remained with her until he died in 1913.

Mrs Greville not only collected people, but also Polesden houses, rare Dutch Old Masters, and Faberge trinkets. She seemed to be less fond of her gardens. Unlike many of the local great estates, Miss Jekyll was not invited to become involved, nor did Miss Willmott's ghost ever appear. However, Mrs Greville's menus are the real masterpieces of Polesden Lacey. For Edward VII, on 6th June 1909, she offered:

consommé à l'impériale
crème ambassadrice
dames de saumon
sauce hollandaise et Genevoise blanchailles
boudins de volaille princesse
selles d'agneau glacées Moscovite
cailles flambées d'ortolans
salade
asperges d'Argenteuil
sauce mousseuse
pêches à la royale
barquettes ecossaises

At the beginning of the new century, the great and the good continued to play a prominent role in Surrey life, but the professional man, and to some extent the professional woman, grew

in importance. On 27th January 1900, Mayor Henry Peak dedi-
cated the new clock of Holy Trinity Church in Guildford High
Street. It played the old chimes of eight bells, and was erected
by public subscription. The Vicar had complained that the old
clock "was altogether too independent to be relied upon".

At noon on Thursday, 9th November 1899, Henry Peak had
been formally elected by the Corporation to be Guildford's
Mayor and Chief Magistrate. After the ceremony, he put on the
scarlet robe and chain of office, and accompanied by the church
bells ringing and crowds cheering, he led the procession of town
worthies to the County and Borough Town Hall, where a
splendid luncheon was ready. As Harry had been born in Stoke-
next-Guildford, he continued taking an interest in the town,
and said the responsibilities of the Mayor "belonged to the
quality and not somebody from nowhere . . . however clever".

When Henry Peak came to power, the Surrey County
Council was just ten years old, and together with the Guildford
Corporation, provided police force, fire brigade, education,
water, sewerage, roads, lighting, etc. The Mayor attended
various committees of the council.

As Mayor, he was ultimately responsible for the town's
20,000 inhabitants and the smooth running of its administra-
tion. As Chief Magistrate, together with the Borough Medical
Officer and Relieving Officer, Mr Peak visited people living in
poor conditions, and members of the community whose sanity
was in doubt and might need to be detained.

When, at the beginning of 1900, there had been terrible
weather and snow lay heavily on the hills above the Wey
Valley, it was Mayor Peak who had to take the responsibility
of sorting everything out. He was forced to react when, on 15th
February, the snows thawed and flooded down into the town.
On 17th February, the floods submerged Messrs Moon's timber
yard on the west side of the river. The contents floated down-
stream, blocking up the arches of the Old Bridge. The town
people were amazed. It had withstood the floods through many

a century, but this time, the waters gushed through and took it with them.

The Mayor immediately established a relief fund to help the victims. However, the matter of the Old Bridge remained complicated and demanded the attention of the Town Council, Surrey County Council, and the River Wey commissioners. Eventually, in 1902, a new bridge made of cast iron and steel was built. Mr Peak complained, "These calamities were a great and extremely powerful strain to me. . . ."

Mr Peak became chair of the governors of Abbot's Hospital (as a senior councillor, he had been previously debarred because he was a Nonconformist), the Royal Grammar School, the Saturday Hospital Fund (raising money for the Royal Surrey County Hospital), and the Indian Famine Relief Fund. He also fundraised for the families of local troops fighting in South Africa.

On 6th May 1910, King Edward VII died. His son George ascended the throne. This was a man Harry *did* approve of. He was a farmer and no-nonsense sailor. Queen Victoria considered the former fiancée of the Duke of Clarence, Princess Victoria Mary of Teck, "a most suitable young woman to be Queen". She encouraged the growing affection between the Duke's younger brother and the Princess. On 6th July 1893, the couple married in Chapel Royal, St James's Palace. They remained devoted to each other. George sent Christmas Cards to "my darling little May" – the family nickname for the Queen, who had been born in that month.

While all these changes in society were going on, Harry and Hannah's family were growing up. Flo had risen to become cook at the Talbot Inn, "the sign of the White Hunting Dog" in the centre of Ripley High Street. In the days of the stage-coach, the Talbot had been one of the most important stopping places en route to Portsmouth. Flo said "it was close enough to London for them to misbehave and far enough away for them to do so." Rumour has it that Nelson and Lady Hamilton spent time together at the Talbot in 1798. The inn is mentioned as far back as the manorial roll of 1580. The 18th-century front conceals a timber-framed structure from at least the early 17th century.

However, Flo's most vivid memory was the shock of seeing a newfangled car entering the archway's large doors, designed for stagecoaches to rattle through and into the courtyard behind. Now inns began to cater for the car. Roads started being tarmacked and thus much easier for cars. The White Lion Inn, Guildford, had eighty rooms and stabling for sixty horses. It began to provide a motor garage and inspection pit. In 1905, an extension for bicycle storage was added.

The Automobile Association began in 1905. For the first few years, the "Motor Scouts" patrolled their areas on bicycles. At first, they wore no uniform, but had AA armbands over a cycling jacket and a large AA badge fixed onto the jacket buttons. In 1909, they were issued with a uniform, and Arthur Nash, the father of a Ripley family, was the AA Motor Scout for the Ripley–Guildford area. Village children remember him calling out "Hurry along now . . . don't be late for school."

A Major Labellier, an eccentric who lived in Dorking, was given to "prophesying". He foresaw that "carriages would one day run without horses." Harry thought such ideas ridiculous and discounted them, especially as the Major had insisted on being buried, at Box Hill on 11th June 1800, upside down.

In the 1911 census, Harry is seventy. He is employed by Surrey County Council as a road labourer. Hannah is seventy-two, and they have one son living with them: Edmund, thirty. He is listed as a garden labourer for the Royal Horticultural Society. Previously, George Hilderley had been courting Kate, the youngest and prettiest of Harry's children. She had married another man, and Flo moved quickly. In October 1910, George and Florence married in St Mary Magdalene's, Ripley. The 1911 census shows the couple living in a cottage in Wisley Gardens, where the laboratory now stands. Flo is twenty-nine, George is twenty-seven. He is a gardener for the RHS, and they have a newborn baby, Charles Henry.

Harry was proud of his children. They could all read and write, and enjoyed "a situation suitable to their position in life". For instance, in 1911, forty-five-year-old Montague was a Post Office worker in Woking. His wife Mary Ann is given as being born in Brighton. Of their children, Clarence, eighteen, is an apprentice to a grocer, Albert, fifteen, is an assistant grocer, and Cecil and Iris are still at school.

After a short illness, Hannah died on 14th April 1912, at the age of seventy-four. She lies in Ripley churchyard. Her stone says simply *Hannah, wife of Henry*, and gives the date of her death.

When Hannah died in 1912, Harry, being born in Stoke near Guildford, was eligible to join the brethren of Abbot's Hospital. The Almshouse stands at the top of Guildford High Street. Jacobean in style, it was built in 1619, during the reign of King James I. Mullioned windows with latticed panes look out over the highest point of the High Street. Turrets stand at each corner, announcing the entrance. The Hospital is a gift to the town from George Abbot, Archbishop of Canterbury, whose birthplace it was. In Harry's day, smoke emerged from the graceful chimneys. In summertime, the quadrangle is still bright with geraniums, but a passage no longer leads to the kitchen garden. Once inside, the visitor becomes aware of the polished oak of staircases, dining hall, boardroom, settles in the old style here and there, and chairs and tables hidden away in alcoves. Some of the windows bear the legend *Calmamus Abba Pater*.

Mostly, relations between Master and brethren were good, but on 8th February 1730, John Hayden abused the Master, *giving him most opprobrious and scurrilous language, giving him the name of fool and bid him to kiss his arse and asking him who made him Master. The Devil he said it was.*

George Abbot lies opposite, in the grandest of Guildford's three churches: the "upper church of Holy Trinity". Born in

1562, he came from an upwardly-mobile family. His father was a Guildford cloth worker. One brother, Robert, became Bishop of Salisbury, and another, Maurice, Mayor of London. Abbot was seen by contemporaries as a narrow-minded Puritan, but he was amongst the learned men who translated the Holy Bible *out of the Original Tongues and with the former Translation diligently compared and revised by His Majesty's special command, AD 1611.* As Archbishop, he crowned King Charles I, and never recovered from accidentally shooting a man with a crossbow. George Abbot died, unmarried, in 1633.

Holy Trinity is the largest Georgian church in Surrey. In 1740, the medieval church collapsed. The congregation "was desirous of improving the church". It had recently been repaired at a cost of £750. When the verger was told that the steeple had collapsed, he replied, "It cannot be. I have the key in my pocket!"

All that remains of the medieval building is the Weston Chapel. The family retained the freehold until 2005, when it was agreed the chapel should come under the jurisdiction of the Church authorities on one condition – once a year, a Catholic Mass should be said. The Onslows had not been forgotten. In 1768, a memorial was erected to Speaker Arthur Onslow, and the 1st Earl and Countess of Onslow presented civic prayer books for the first service taking place in the new church.

The Onslows would not know, and neither would Harry, that the next chapter of their lives would be so different. Harry's Mr Gladstone had warned about the growing *dreadful military spirit.* The world was about to become a terrible place, but despite it all, Miss Jekyll could say, "the scent of the year's first primrose is no small pleasure . . . ."

CHAPTER SEVEN

1914–1930

Winter before Spring

On 28th July 1914, the Great War began. At first, it had little impact on Harry, who thought it would be all over by Christmas, but he did agree with George V: "Grand-mama would never have allowed it." For the first time in his life, Harry found himself living alone, not even with a cat for company. Flo was busy in Wisley looking after George and their newborn baby Charlie. On 4th August 1914, the 5th Battalion of the Queen's Royal West Surrey Regiment paraded through Guildford. It was then that Guildfordians learned "England has declared war on Germany." George said to Flo, "It's but a five-minute wonder, Gal." Nevertheless, many of his friends rushed off to enlist. Special constables volunteered to take the place of the police officers who had gone to the war. Civilian sentries stood guard on the bridges around Guildford, among them the High Sheriff of Surrey, Mr J. H. Bridges, and Lord Onslow. Horse owners offered their horses for the war effort, and received 5/- per animal.

People panicked, fearing food shortages. Harry and Flo did not. They were country people and always knew where to find food. Early in the mornings, shopkeepers opened their doors to find long queues forming outside. In 1915, Guildford was shaken to see a Zeppelin hovering over the town. Ten bombs fell close to St Catherine's, killing seventeen fowls and a swan. A year later, there was even greater consternation when bakers announced "we have no ingredients to make hot-cross buns." A

Relief Committee was formed, providing food and clothes. In 1918, notices appeared on butchers' shops. Residents were horrified to read, "Sold out."

The great houses opened their doors to become nursing and convalescent homes; even the Royal County Hospital offered to care for the wounded. When the Germans invaded Belgium, many Guildfordians welcomed the refugees into their own homes. As soon as war was announced, the 5th Earl of Onslow became a special constable. He organised the gardeners at Clandon to bridge watch and instructed the villagers to destroy any strong alcohol they possessed "in case of invasion". His Lordship upset one strong-minded lady. She was insulted that he thought she kept strong drink in the house. Later, Lord Onslow organised the Red Cross operation, transporting and caring for wounded soldiers. Subsequently, he became an intelligence officer and ended the war as colonel-in-charge of censorship and publicity in France. His Lordship was awarded the Légion d'honneur in recognition of his work. After the war, he became Undersecretary of State for War, Privy Councillor, and chaired various committees in the House of Lords.

With the outbreak of war, the Onslows offered Clandon Park as a military hospital serving all ranks. The majority of rooms were used as wards, including the grand marble entrance hall. Nurses were billeted on the second floor; operations were carried out in Lord Onslow's dressing room. The men usually arrived directly from the battlefield, "shattered and half starved". Lady Onslow was appointed Commandant, in charge of the Voluntary Aid Detachment working at Clandon and two other nearby houses, Broom House at West Horsley, and Heywood at Cobham. She wore her uniform in public, which only "people of the lower orders" and suffragettes did. Her mother's friends ignored her. Officers pushed her to one side rushing for taxis. Her ladyship called out, "Sir, you are not a gentleman!"

However, a small girl in Cobham did know what a gentleman was. One morning, she was late for school and had to collect the family's pail of milk from the Home Farm. Marjorie waited anxiously as rows and rows of soldiers marched past. Then an officer approached, mounted on a horse. He held up his hand and stopped his men. She crossed the lane and curtsied. He saluted her, and "that," she told her daughter, "was a real gentleman."

During the Great War, 5,059 soldiers were admitted to Clandon, and 747 operations carried out. Due to the serious injuries of many of the soldiers, and the "Spanish flu" epidemic of 1918, the house remained a hospital until April 1919. When the last soldier was discharged, the men presented Lady Onslow with a silver salt cellar as a "thank you". By the end of the war, Lady Onslow's health had declined, and she spent most of her time with her brother at his Devon estate.

In the early days of the 20th century, people had little understanding of mental illness. A soldier's physical injuries were cared for, but not his mental wounds. On 19th November 1914, just as the war was beginning, the first Mayor of Guildford, Henry Peak, died in Holloway Sanatorium at Virginia Water. This was a new idea in hospitals, designed for people of the middle to upper-middle classes suffering from nervous diseases such as dementia. It was the pet project of the patent-medicine millionaire Thomas Holloway. Building began in 1873, and was not completed until 1885. His wife Jane also had a brilliant thought – an all-women's college. Holloway built it in the same style, close to the Sanatorium. Although later generations considered Holloway's medicine dubious, he was an establishment figure who donated vast sums of money to various philanthropic causes. As a mark of society's esteem, Queen Victoria opened the Royal Holloway College in 1886, and it became a constituent college of the University of London in 1900.

Holloway did not live to see either building completed. He died at the age of eighty-three in 1883. Like Harry, he did not trust doctors or lawyers. Holloway also loathed parsons, which

Harry did not. He owed much of his success to clever advertising, spending £50,000 a year on promoting his pills. After Holloway's death, the business slowly declined and was eventually purchased by his rival, Thomas Beecham. However, the two buildings he built "as a gift to the nation" remain.

Henry Peak remembered several institutions in his will, including the Royal Surrey County Hospital. However, a resident of Guildford commented, "Henry Peak gave three generations of his fellow citizens a modest and humane environment – which seems an honourable epitaph."

Like so many people, the Great War changed Flo and George's lives. In 1915, he led twelve lads up the lane to go to war. Reluctantly, George joined the East Kent Regiment, "the Buffs". Four years later, he came back down the lane – alone. He never entered a church again, except for his own funeral. Harry knew Flo would need support, and moved into her small back box-bedroom. Harry was amazed to find the privy was indoors. He had brought with him the *London Illustrated News*' Diamond Jubilee portrait of Queen Victoria (on silk). Flo placed it in an oak frame and hung it over the parlour fireplace. On the mantelpiece, Harry placed a photograph of Mr Gladstone with "Dossie", his granddaughter, sitting on his knee. They appeared to be gazing upwards, in awe, at the old Queen. However, if you looked carefully, you would see they were looking at a robin perched on a branch. In the kitchen, Harry placed a glass case which Hannah had loved so. It contained a white stuffed owl; in its claw, it held a field mouse. To the right of the kitchen range, he placed Hannah's Windsor chair, puffing up the knitted cushion she had made for it. He then solemnly entered the parlour and put the great Bible on a delicate bamboo table.

For George, like many men, the war remained a "dark period" not to be discussed. During the first few days of arriving in the barracks, George wrote to Flo complaining about "rations and the state of the food". Fortunately, he was let off with a caution. The following year (1916), the Regiment went to Ireland to quell the Easter Uprising being fought in Dublin's Post Office. George was shocked by the way the Irish lived and the casual attitude of the absentee landlords. Within six days, the uprising was over and the leaders executed. Back in Wisley, Harry muttered about Mr Gladstone and Home Rule. In 1917, George was shipped abroad and saw action in France. He was taken prisoner, and beaten so badly for insubordination that he suffered back pain for the rest of his life. On her fourteenth birthday, George gave his granddaughter a book, *All Quiet on the Western Front*, so she would know, when the next war came, what she was sending her boys to.

Eventually, *on the 11ᵗʰ hour of the 11ᵗʰ day of the 11ᵗʰ month*, "the war to end all wars" came to an end. Harry rang the bell of St Mary's church, announcing it was all over – except, in reality, it was not. On 25ᵗʰ January 1919, soldiers returned to Guildford. They travelled by train and marched through cheering crowds from the station to the Guildhall, but nearly 500 of their number did not. An A. C. Worsfold appears on the memorial in Ripley churchyard. He may have been one of Harry's sons – if so, he was never mentioned. On the morning of 2ⁿᵈ July 1919, the High Sheriff, Mr J. H. Bridges, stood on the steps of Holy Trinity and read the official declaration of peace.

When George returned to Wisley, he found a modern research laboratory had replaced his cottage. Now Flo, Charlie, and Harry lived at No. 5 The Square. In 1915, the RHS had built six houses around a square in the Surrey style, bordering the fruit fields. All their neighbours worked for the Society, including Mrs Knight. Each spring, she produced a baby; by the autumn, it had joined all the others in the churchyard. Now Wisley no longer consisted *of a few scattered farms and cottages*; it had become a community, with a village shop which sold gobstoppers, tobacco, and bottles of Guinness – everything, in fact, even postage stamps.

Flo was amazed to find she possessed both a front door and back door, which led into a scullery with a copper and a larder.

In the kitchen, she found a range, windows that opened onto the garden, and a bay window that overlooked the square. However, she did complain that with the post-war shortage of coal, the cottage was difficult to keep warm. There was a built-in dresser on which she placed her best red-and-gold-decorated dinner and tea service "bought" with cigarette coupons. There was even enough room for a large ornate sideboard which housed all her pink glass. In the middle of the room stood an oak table with an oil lamp proudly in its centre.

On the mantle, Flo placed the slate clock. Plants blossomed on every windowsill. Decorating the walls were Helen Allingham prints of pretty cottages. In the parlour, a chaise lounge divided the room into two. Spindly chairs and bamboo tables added an additional sense of refinement. This room would only be used for "high days, holidays, and funerals".

Upstairs, there were three bedrooms. In the master bedroom stood a giant bed with a goose-feather mattress. Every day she polished its brass surrounds. On the mahogany washstand, Flo placed a rose-covered jug and bowl. The chamber pot had the same decorations. In the corners, she placed the china fairings that George had won at the country fairs. Charlie tried to understand the two little china figures which sat in a bed looking longingly at each other. At the bottom of the bed was inscribed the words, "Now dear or later?" His parents never explained it to him. The little boy stood open-mouthed when he saw his own bedroom. It had a double bed, a washstand, and a bookcase. There was room for books and toys and all manner of things. The room looked out over the vegetable garden. He could climb down the tree, whose branches tapped at his window, and once down he could run around the garden without once disturbing his parents.

As the dreadful war was finally coming to an end, the Ministry of Food was still making sure that the harvest from the hedgerows was not wasted, and on 21st September 1918, the Ripley school logbook records, "At the request of the Ministry of Food, and with the consent of the Managers, groups of children are being sent out to gather blackberries." They collected 108 pounds, which was probably made into jam. Charlie enjoyed bread and jam for tea, especially if it was strawberry jam.

When the war loomed into becoming a reality, the country began calling for volunteers to join the fight. The Ripley school logbook records that "in May 1915, the military hurriedly took over this school for military purposes." The occupation lasted four days, and then the school returned to its normal routine. Over one hundred young men from Ripley joined the forces and saw service: Walter Sidney Smythe, a young teacher who had been employed at the school for two years, joined up in 1914; the Vicar of Ripley left in 1915 to become a chaplain to the Navy; and in 1917, Mr Blaxland, the headmaster, went to the war, leaving Mr R. H. Green in temporary charge. All three men survived the war, but twenty-eight men from Ripley did not.

However, the health of the school children was giving concern. In 1914, Surrey Education Committee set up a School Care Committee in every school in the county, *whose duty will be the health of the children whilst at school; that is, medical inspection followed by medical treatment at low cost to the parents.* The Ripley Care Committee discussed the best means of raising money to carry out the recommendations of the inspectorate with regards to adenoids, tonsils, eyes, and teeth.

The fees were as follows:

- adenoids, including stay at clinic hospital = £1 6s 0d
- for teeth, from 1s 6d
- for eyes, to include two visits = 10s 6d
- for spectacles, from 7s 6d

The Ripley magazine reported that *the Committee have agreed to ask parents to subscribe at least a half-penny a week, when possible one penny, and to send the money each Monday morning to the Head Teacher. Those parents who do not subscribe regularly will get no assistance from Surrey Education Committee or from Ripley Care Committee. The parents that do will not be called upon to pay anything further towards the fees.*

By 1918, the Ripley Care Committee was giving cod-liver oil, Maltine, and Easton's syrup on medical recommendation, "but only to parents whose parents subscribed regularly". Charlie attended Byfleet School, and remembered swallowing cod-liver oil and being told "it is good for you!"

In December 1915, the children of Ripley school, during the holidays, gave a concert to raise money on behalf of the war fund. In the autumn of 1917, they collected two tons of horse chestnuts for the Ministry of Munitions, for use as animal food.

Flo had not enjoyed being an independent woman. On the other hand, she may have come across a young Jewish woman who did enjoy her independence, except for wedding anniversaries. "They are not much fun without a husband," said Mrs Helen Bentwich (née Franklin), a member of the wealthy Jewish banking family. She had just married Norman, a brilliant young lawyer, who had left for the Middle East. Left alone, Helen needed occupation and called to see the Home Secretary, Uncle Herbert Samuel.

She asked him, "What can I do to aid the war effort?" He offered her a nice little office job. She refused it, and found herself a job in The Arsenal at Woolwich. On 11th September 1916, she wrote to Norman: *Coming into the Arsenal at 7 a.m. is like going into a huge fair. Crowds of people, mainly women, jostling and pushing . . . mixed up with strings of WD lorries, and trains careering madly . . . and outside the Arsenal gates ice-cream, milk and cheap sweet vendors galore . . . one girl coming from the canteen fell into a vat of boiling water and was killed. At the inquest the Arsenal was censured for gross negligence; but it had no effect.*

She wrote in her diary, *London, 5th January 1917. My birthday. I'm twenty five, which seems awfully old ... I've written about condi-*

*tions to every Ministry in the least concerned, but nothing has happened.
London, 4th April 1917. I've got the sack!*

Helen returned to Uncle Samuel. He advised her to "keep
to a nice, little office job". Instead, she bought a motorbike
and joined the Women's Land Army. Helen became group
leader for the Home Counties. Her job was to persuade farmers to employ land girls, who were often alarmed to see a
young woman wearing trousers. The government had warned:
*You are doing a man's work and so you are dressed rather like a man:
but remember because you wear a smock and trousers you are to take
care to behave like an English girl who expects chivalry and respect
from everyone she meets.*

She found that not all farmers behaved well, but she said of
"one dear old farmer of eighty . . . finally said he would take a
girl for three weeks for the harvest . . . he refused to change the
time, and talked of that damned maggoty government in
London." Another place was run by a rich widow: "She gave me
lots of strawberries and cream. I got home quite late again."

Sometimes Helen found herself helping the girls. She
continued writing to Norman: *8th May 1917. I've been spreading
muck all day, and it's a mucky job.* In October, she told him *I
collected a potato gang for a farmer from the slums of Hertford. They
are very bad slums, and a lot of the families are 'rag-pickers', and the
rags are piled in the rooms where they live. I believe that the worst slums
are in the towns around the large estates. . . .* On 26th November
1917, Helen wrote, *Food is getting as much of a problem as petrol.
Often I can't get meals at pubs or tea-shops, as they say they have run
out, and I am getting very hungry.* By 1918, sugar, meat, butter,
cheese, and margarine were rationed. At that time, Helen
Bentwich did not expect to become a Labour politician or Chair
of the London County Council and receive numerous invitations
to speak. However, on 6th December 1917, she wrote to Norman
that *next week I'm to make a speech in the village, because they are
forming a new organization called a Women's Institute, and I'm to be
the star turn, which rather alarms me.*

By December 1918, the Great War was over, and Helen sailed on an Orient liner to meet Norman. *After a few days in Cairo we travelled to Jerusalem to begin our new life together.*

When George returned home, he brought his rifle with him. A crack shot, he said, "whether it is man or beast you kill, you do it quick and clean." Unlike Harry, he did not approve of or follow the hunt. Charlie told the story of one morning when he was with his father in Wisley churchyard. They heard the sound of the hunt approaching. "Watch," said George. Through the hedge crept an old fox. He ran round the gravestones and into the church porch, hiding behind some wooden logs. Soon the hunt came galloping across the fields. For a moment, the hounds lost the scent. "That way," called out George, pointing towards Byfleet. When it was all clear, the old fox emerged. For a few minutes, man and beast looked at each other. Then, with a hop and skip, the fox ran off London way, in the opposite direction.

Early in the war, George's brother John had enlisted in the Coldstream Guards. Almost immediately, he was invalided out and never recovered his strength. After the war, their eldest brother Charles returned to Berkshire, where he was born. He was one of the troops who, on Christmas day, sang carols with the enemy, exchanged cigarettes, and enjoyed a game of football. Charles became friendly with a young German. The next day, he killed him.

Following the War, Charles joined the outdoor staff of Bishopsgate House, Windsor. Soon he became head gardener, growing things and debating with Queen Mary, whom he held in the highest regard. Her Majesty visited the gardens and suggested plants which should grow in the greenhouses. "Don't you agree Mr Hilderley?"

"It's not for me to agree or disagree, ma'am."

"Mr Hilderley, you must have an opinion."

"I bow to your judgement, ma'am."

A few months later, the couple would look down on a tray of wilting plants. "Of course, they die," muttered Flo, "if you don't water them." Occasionally, Uncle Charles let the Queen win. He would repeat, "I bow to your judgement, ma'am."

"Quite so Mr Hilderley," the Queen would say, with just a hint of a smile.

However, the royal family did allow his daughter Phyllis to marry in the Chapel Royal, and invited him and his family to Windsor Castle to a private viewing of the Queen's dolls' house.

Like many women, Queen Mary loved miniatures. Princess Marie-Louise, one of Queen Victoria's granddaughters, recounted how one day she came across the Queen furnishing a dolls' house. The Princess asked Lutyens, "Ned, will you design a dolls' house fit for a Queen?" He laughed and pushed the remark to one side. Some time later, he said, "I have been thinking about your suggestion. Let us devise and design something which for all time will enable future generations to see how a King and Queen of England lived in the 20th century, and what authors, artists and craftsmen of note there were during that reign."

From 1921 to 1924, Lutyens designed a dolls' house that Queen Mary "could feel she could wander around in and feel at home". The building is on a scale of one inch to the foot, and over three feet tall. Some 1,500 artists, craftsmen, and manufacturers contributed to it. Some of the replicas are copies of items to be found in Windsor Castle: a cradle in the nursery waits for baby, four-poster beds require grand people to sleep in them, copper pans in the kitchen shine with loving care, the grand piano in the salon shows the owners to be cultured folk; the long dining table is set with glass, silver cutlery, and gold dishes, waiting for a banquet to be served. Even the bottles of wine in the cellar are filled with the appropriate wine. The shotguns break and load, lavatories flush, and light fittings work. The carpets, curtains, and furnishings are all copies of the real things, and there is even a strongroom with miniature Crown Jewels. In the library, tiny books by writers such as Rudyard

Kipling, M. R. James, and Somerset Maugham line the shelves. Only George Bernard Shaw and Sir Edgar Elgar refused to contribute.

The drawers beneath the house hide an ornamental garden designed by Miss Jekyll. Rustic seats are set against walls, poplars surround the Georgian exterior, and trimmed lawns invite one to sit down and relax. Charlie was delighted with the small cars, well-polished and ready for chauffeurs to drive them away. Flo looked at the house wonderingly. "I only had a rag doll to play with, and that was a hand-me-down!" The Queen's dolls' house was displayed at the Empire Exhibition in 1921, and seen by over a million people. Following the exhibition, it went on display in Windsor Castle to raise funds for Queen Mary's charities.

There were no stables in the Queen's dolls' house, nor huntsmen either. All through the war years, the hunt had struggled to survive. In 1914, the Surrey Union Hunt's expenses amounted to £2,549 15 5d, and income of £2,047 9 0d. There was a shortage of members because so many country men had volunteered to join the Army, and the hunters were requisitioned as "they make ideal chargers for officers". In December 1915, the War Office expressed the desire that "the hunt, if possible, continue partly because the fox population need to be kept down because they steal desperately needed poultry". The Army appreciated "the breeding and raising of light horses suitable for cavalry work". However, by the spring of 1917, the German U-boat blockade was beginning to bite. The enemy submarines were blocking the Allies' trade routes bringing essential food and raw materials to Britain. The Board of Trade placed restrictions on animal foodstuffs and "thought was given to killing off unessential hounds". Only by the skin of its teeth did the Surrey Union Hunt survive the Great War. However, when the sun was setting, the hunt still came down Wisley Lane. The younger huntsmen would lean down, saying, "Come on up, youngster." The children sat astride the horses until they arrived at the end of the village. Then the huntsmen put them down and they ran back to their mothers.

Even Mrs Greville had been touched by the war. During 1915, she converted her golf course into a potato patch, exhorted her gardeners to grow more food, and opened the north and west wings of Polesden Lacey as a convalescent home for soldiers. In the August of 1915, King George V and Queen Mary visited the home. There is a story that when the Queen was visiting another such establishment, a member of her entourage complained, "I am tired and hate hospitals." Her Majesty snapped, "You are a member of the Royal family. We are never tired, and we love hospitals." After the War, Mrs Greville returned to her old ways, entertaining royalty and celebrities with equal brilliance, and not even becoming discomforted when George V and Queen Mary telephoned at short notice, inviting themselves to tea. On the other hand, Mrs Greville was very much annoyed when the hunt rode across her lands. Immediately she called her agents, Cluttons, instructing them to demand compensation.

A man whom Mrs Greville would have enjoyed entertaining was George Sutherland-Leveson-Gower, 5th Duke of Sutherland, KT, PC. In 1919, he bought nearby Sutton Place and lived there for the next forty-four years, during which time he modernised the interior. He said of Sutton Place, "It is large enough to be dignified and small enough to be comfortable." In his twenties, "Geordie" had been the greatest landowner in the British Isles. He possessed a private train and owned a coalmine. A navvy is supposed to have said, "That's wot I call a real Dook, there's 'e driving his own engine, of his own train, and a-burning his own bloody coal."

The 5th Duke had a military background, and from 1914 was an honorary colonel of the 5th Battalion of the Seaforth Highlanders. During the war, he took a commission in the Royal Naval Reserve and rose to the rank of Commander. He held senior appointments in the Conservative administrations of Andrew Bonar Law and Stanley Baldwin, and is remembered as patron of the British film industry, with the Sutherland Trophy named in his honour.

Ripley remembers him as a good-looking man who had an eye for a pretty woman. He married twice: in 1891, to Lady Eileen Butler, and later to Clare Josephine O'Brian. There were no children from either marriage, but Barbara Cartland suspected he was the father of her daughter Raine, Princes Diana's stepmother.

As Surrey remained a hunting county well into the 20th century, it may have been impressed by the Duke's boast that he shot his first stag at the age of ten. It would not have approved of the way he searched the world for big game – not for food or because it was vermin, but for the pleasure of killing. He said he loved bringing down a giant elephant and watching it die. When a friend collapsed on a shoot, he observed, "Personally, I can think of no pleasanter way to die."

Sutton Place was always to be in wealthy hands, but in 1919, the Lovelace estate fell on hard times. The 3rd Earl, much to Harry's distress, decided to sell Horsley Towers. From 1914, the aircraft designer, aviator, and yachtsman lived in Compton House. It was one of the first houses to be built on Cobham's prestigious Fairmile Estate. "Tommy" Sopwith rented shooting rights from the Earl, and it was thought he wanted to buy Horsley Towers. The property possessed 250 acres of parkland, and it was suspected Sopwith wished to erect an aerodrome on it. It is believed that he made an offer of £200,000 before the public sale. The rent roll amounted to £2,500, excluding the Lovelace seat. The estimated value of the timber alone was put between £64,000 and £80,000.

Mr Sopwith sold Compton House to Philip Lyle of the sugar-refining firm, and in 1920, bought Horsley Towers. He paid £150,000 for it. At ten years of age, Sopwith had accidentally shot his father, and subsequently inherited great wealth. He bought an aeroplane, went to Brooklands airfield, and taught himself to fly. Sopwith had been a disaster at school, but from his earliest years, was "terribly bitten by the aviation bug". In 1910, he took delivery of his first aircraft, a Bleriot-inspired Avis monoplane. He said, "we had lots of crashes in those days but, bless you, it was fun. When it was all over, we nearly always just stood up, shook the wreckage off and walked away." The nearby sewerage farm was always hazard for a trainee pilot. It was claimed that no man could be considered an aviator unless he had taken a toss into it.

Nevertheless, Sopwith quit the air for a ground-based management and design role. In 1912, "Tommy" formed the Sopwith Aviation Company, based at Kingston-upon-Thames. In August 1914, Brooklands and all its services, including the racetrack, were taken over by the War Office, who formed a military flying school. After the outbreak of the First World War, the "Tabloid" was the first aircraft which Sopwith sold to the military, but the aeroplane with which he will always be remembered is the "Camel", an agile and highly manoeuvrable machine that shot down more Germans than any other. The Sopwith Aviation Company was even more prolific than the Vickers Aircraft Works. They employed 5,000, and made 16,000 aircraft. Vickers Armstrong started manufacturing aircraft in 1915, and with a growing number of military contracts, had to extend their Byfleet premises. By the time the war ended, Vickers had built some 4,500 aircraft of different designs. The company built a housing estate in Byfleet to accommodate their workforce, who often did not have enough to eat. Women increasingly replaced men, and after the war, they would find difficulty in returning to their traditional roles.

By 1916, there was a shortage of wheat, and thus of bread, but with government interventions, nobody starved. The rich used the black market, and during August there had been panic as food became more of a problem. After the First World War, perhaps because of Vickers Armstrong, Byfleet was among the first parish councils to install street lighting, improve recreation facilities, and start to campaign for better housing and sanitation.

It was said a new recruit had a greater chance of being killed during training than in combat. At the beginning of the Great War, one unknown British general said, "The airplane is useless for the purposes of war." By November 1918, the "flying machines" bore little resemblance to the lightweight craft flown at the beginning of the war. The Royal Flying Corps no longer existed. It had become the Royal Air Force, and the men and their officers were no longer part of the British Army. Aircraft brought with them a new strategy which put civilians at risk. Now aircraft could target the armament factories and eventually, to Harry's horror, bomb unknown thousands.

However, when the war was over, aeroplane sales crashed, and by 1920 Sopwith's company had no prospect of receiving any large military contracts. The Treasury went after him for excessive war profits. Sopwith paid off all his creditors, and the company went into voluntary liquidation. The grounds at Horsley Towers were divided up and sold off. Nevertheless, Tommy bounced back. He married twice, and eventually owned estates in Hampshire, Yorkshire, and the Isle of Harris. On 27th January 1989, Sir Thomas Octave Murdoch Sopwith, CBE, died. He was 101.

By 1920, the Lovelaces had left Surrey, never to return. Harry was saddened. He felt the 3rd Earl had not lived up to his father's great reputation and was not worthy to bear his name. Harry was now nearly eighty. Like Miss Jekyll, he considered the changes brought about by the Great War "did not suit".

Harry had spent the past few years living with George, Flo, and Charlie. Although he was over seventy and of good character, through working he was not eligible to receive Lloyd George's old-age pension of 5/- per week. The Act was passed in 1908, and was means tested. The amount was set low to encourage people to continue working and make provision for their old age. Harry preferred to remain independent even though it meant repairing the roads. The work brought him in more than £31 10 0d. By 1919, the pension had been increased to ten shillings a week, which he received from the Ripley Post Office. Unlike many of his contemporaries, he understood forms and could write his signature (not making a cross) in order to receive the money. Harry received additional help from the West Surrey Benefit Society, and paid Flo "in full for his board and lodging".

The routine of the household continued as before the war. As dawn approached, George and Flo would get out of bed. The kitchen fire was lit, the kettle placed on it. Flo put a packet of "Force" on the table. George shook the flakes out into a bowl, swamping them with milk. They consisted of "such goodness as wheat, malt, dash of salt and sugar". "Sunny Jim" on the packet promised "Vigour, Vim and Perfect Trim". Flo had bought the doll. He was propped up in the scullery, elegant in hat, pony-tail, high-collar jacket, narrow Regency-style trousers, and spats. In the newspapers, "Sunny Jim" advertised "Force Flakes", announcing, "High o'er the fence leaps Sunny Jim, Force is the food that raises him."

Next, Flo poured George a cup of tea out of the brown teapot. She put it back on the griddle before the fire. It would remain there until bedtime, topped up during the day with extra tea leaves and water from the kettle. This remained whistling away gently on the range. At 8 a.m., George returned to eat a full English breakfast. Charlie would join him before going to school. At 9 a.m., Harry emerged. He considered it to be the greatest luxury of his life "eating breakfast at nearly dinner time". At 11 a.m., he stepped out and went down the lane, passing the church and continuing on until he reached the Anchor Inn at Pyford Lock, a good three miles away. Here he would greet mates, discuss the matters of the day, sip a pint or two, puff at his pipe, and watch the narrowboats travelling along the canal and the traffic going over the narrow hump-backed bridge.

Harry started back down the lane for dinner at 1:30 p.m. After the meal, George placed the *Daily Express* over his face and snoozed. Flo sat quietly. At the first signs of stirrings from her husband, she poured him a cup of tea. After sipping the mixture, George returned to work and Harry climbed the stairs for a lay down. Sometimes, he wandered back down the lane to two RHS cottages to take tea with Granny Powell. She was an elderly widow, almost as old as Harry. They had been children together in Ripley. In the spring of 1922, she told him she was to start another family. The husband of her niece, Kate Smith, had been shot on the Somme. Following an unsuccessful operation for an ulcer, she had died in Cobham Cottage Hospital, leaving behind her three children. "They either come to me or go into the workhouse, Harry." Will, fifteen, Marjorie, thirteen, and Ted, eleven, came to live with the old woman.

"I haven't the money, Marge, for you to become a teacher, and I doubt if the Combes will pay now you have come to live here," she told the girl. "You will have to go into Service." Will was a hunchback and could not do manual work, but was bright. He went to work in the laboratory as a clerk, recording new plants. Ted went with Charlie to Byfleet School. In 1925, when he left at fourteen, he worked for the "Gardens". Marjorie saved as much money as she could and bought Ted an apprenticeship. He became a master carpenter.

"Marge" worked hard and soon became "Nanny Smith", never applying for a position, but making it known when her charges no longer needed her. While being interviewed, a potential employer dreaded to hear that "I don't think we would be suited, Madam." Nanny Smith arrived with baby, and stayed until the child went to prep school. She insisted on a strict routine and a little maid for the hard work. At five o'clock, the children were washed and dressed. They were taken down to the drawing room, where the little girls curtsied to Mama and Papa and were kissed. The little boys shook hands with Papa and were pecked on the forehead by Mama. There was one dreadful time when Madam arrived in the nursery — she wished to play with her own children.

At some point, Nanny Smith applied to train as a Norland Nanny. She terrified them half to death when explaining her philosophy of childcare: "It's either baby or me." A rather weak male was told, "Vicar, it's easy to control toddlers. You just catch the eye." Nanny Smith observed that "on no account should Nanny become 'soppy' about the children." However, when she died, her family discovered a drawer full of knick-knacks and cards signed "To Nanny with Love."

While Harry's working life was coming to an end, George's blossomed. In 1923, as *the master propagator and pruner of fruit trees*, he was appointed foreman of the RHS Fruit Farm, and later took control of the National Fruit Trials. When George entered the laboratory, he would see on the north wall of the entrance hall a bronze panel erected in 1921. On it are listed the names of the twenty students who were killed in the Great War. He knew them, every one. To celebrate his promotion, and perhaps his survival from the war, he bought Flo and Charlie a wind-up oak gramophone with cabinet and room for numerous His Master's Voice records. Charlie especially liked "Nipper", the little terrier whose ears were cocked listening to his master's voice. Harry thought listening to sounds made without instruments was unnatural.

The editor of *Gardens Club Journal* wrote, in 1922, *I believe that the fruit-growing industry is on the eve of very great developments, the result of which will add materially to the prestige of horticulture.* Horticultural experts came to the fruit fields seeking George's opinion. Many of the great and the good lived locally, like H. G. Wells and Arthur Conan Doyle, and chatted to him. George was a very sensible and presentable man, and politicians like David Lloyd George used him as a sounding board. They all received the same answer: "Ha, You may be right, Sir." A special favourite was RHS committee member David Bowes-Lyon's sister, Elizabeth. George called her simply "Ma'am", while Flo referred to her as "George's Lady".

In 1925, Charlie left school. He was fourteen, and Harry reminded him that "I was ten when I had to go out to work." He joined his father in the "Gardens", but soon bought himself a bicycle and rode into Ripley to learn how to drive and care for a car. In 1927, he announced to his startled parents that "I'm to be a gentleman's gentleman." Charlie became valet-chauffeur to Mr Alfred Ezra, OBE, of Foxwarren Park, a Gothic-style house near Cobham. E. H. Shepherd used it to illustrate Toad Hall in *Wind in the Willows*, and it has been described as "big and violent with crow-stepped gables".

Two years later, after Charlie joined Mr Ezra, a widowed, wealthy bishop came to stay. He wished to own a Rolls-Royce, and asked Charlie's advice. He suggested a Rolls-Royce Phantom, in suitable black, and bought one for the old gentleman. The body had to be made by a coachbuilder chosen by the owner. Charlie's advice was sought. He recommended Thrupp and Maberly, mainly because they were in the West End. The Bishop was impressed by Charlie and the company, who were involved with the Coachbuilders' Benevolent Institute. Eventually, this became BEN, the charity for the automotive and related industries. The Bishop invited Charlie to be his "gentleman's gentleman". The two glided around the countryside, only "buses daring to get in their way", and Charlie discovered Brooklands.

In the early years of the 20th century, racing on roads was forbidden. A relative of the Earls of Lovelace, Hugh Fortescue Locke King, inherited from his father, MP Peter John Locke King, an estate at Weybridge. It consisted of marshy land which supported only sheep and crops. If motor racing was ever to compete with Europe, Locke King decided that Britain must have its own racing track and embarked on a European tour to discover how to make a motor-racing course. On his return to Surrey, he spent over £150,000 of his own money to build a track, and called it "Brooklands" after the name of his house.

The world's first banked motor-racing circuit took place at Brooklands in 1906. The motoring press enthused about it. In December 1906, the Brooklands Automobile Racing Club was formed and was officially opened on 17th June 1907. The diarist Lady Mary Monkswell wrote, in July, *Mr and Mrs Locke King came to dinner. They have been building this awful motor track and are so hated by their neighbours . . . that hardly anyone will speak to them.*

On 15th February 1913, Percy (Pearly) Lambert was the first person to exceed one hundred miles an hour, driving a 4.5-litre side-valve Talbot 103 miles and 1,470 yards in an hour! On 21st October 1913, he attempted a further record. A tyre burst. As the car burst into a ball of flames, Lambert was thrown onto the track. He died en route to Weybridge Cottage Hospital. Less than two weeks later, he had been due to marry his fiancée and give up motor racing. People say they have seen a figure speeding round the track. A security guard saw and heard "a swirling blackness and the horrendous sound of crashing and splintering near the shed". Despite such setbacks, the motoring press continued to enthuse about "Brooklands", and young men like Charlie flocked to the racetrack.

A favourite meeting place for young "swells" was the Hut Hotel. It was in the centre of a part of the Portsmouth Road running between Kingston-upon-Thames and Guildford. It was a lonely spot by the side of Lake Bolder Mere, surrounded by bleak heathlands. The hotel stood on the site of the old Hut. In such a spot, an inn was a welcome place and a favourite haunt of highwaymen, especially Jerry Abershawe. He was a jolly, courteous rogue known as the "Laughing Highwayman". There is a story that he was taken ill at the Bald-faced Stag Inn in Putney Vale. The innkeeper sent to Kingston for a doctor. The highwayman begged him not to travel back alone so late at night, and offered him his protection. The doctor tossed the offer aside: "I fear no one, not even Abershawe himself."

For several years, the highwayman evaded the Bow Street Runners, but in January 1795, they caught him after he shot one of them dead. Jerry Abershawe was hung on 3rd August 1793. He was only twenty-two or -three years old, and remains something of a local folk hero, remembered for mimicking the judge at his trial and exchanging badinage with the crowds as he made his way to the gallows. After his death, his body was displayed as a warning to others on Putney Common. He was the last highwayman to suffer such an indignity. Passers-by removed his finger and toe bones, wishing to keep them as souvenirs.

Aberhawe's ghost does not haunt the Portsmouth Road, but there are many that do. A young girl may still be seen standing on the site of the Old Tartar Inn at Cobham. It is always late at night, and rain is falling heavily. A driver stops. She climbs into the back of the car, staring straight ahead, saying nothing. The girl gives no destination, but when the driver arrives in Church Street, she opens the car door. He offers her his mackintosh. She places it around her shoulders and turns to him, "I will leave it for you." The man drives on, going along the Portsmouth Road. When he returns, he passes the churchyard. He sees the mackintosh lying across an unmarked grave that belongs to a young girl burned to death long ago when the old Tartar Inn caught fire.

Charlie and the old Bishop did not go to the Hut, but occasionally Charlie caught the train to London. He loved to wander around the City and Fleet Street. Before coming home, he would call into Frank Matcham's Coliseum, *the largest and finest people's palace for entertainment of the age*, the London Palladium, or the Palace Theatre of Varieties and watch the *tableux vivante* – young ladies appearing in the nude (actually, covered with "fleshings", flesh-toned body stockings).

Charlie returned to Surrey by the unpleasantly-nicknamed "Stiffs' Express". He made sure he looked suitably mournful. The Necropolis line was opened in 1854, despite objections, to take coffins and mourners from Waterloo to funerals in Surrey. The London and South-Western Railway (LSWR) built a branch line running off the main line with two stations: one for members of the Church of England, and the other for Nonconformists, Turks, Jews, infidels, and heathens. Brookwood station opened into the grounds of the 2,000-acre cemetery owned by the London Necropolis Company. Initially, the company hoped to make at least £40,000 a year and solve London's burial problem. Charlie preferred to travel first class, but many penny-pinching golfers travelling to nearby West Hill Golf Club did not. Each train was divided into first-, second-, and third-class compartments, but during the 1930s, demand for the service dropped.

Miss Jekyll preferred to travel by pony and governess cart. By the time the war had ended, she was over seventy. Her sight had worsened, and she felt she was growing old. The cost of living remained high, and she had no children to look after or care for her, but she felt responsible for her staff and her cats. They had been with her for many, many years. She wrote to a friend in April 1919: *what happens to an old woman does not really matter and if it must be, I shall face it quite cheerfully as my way of paying for the war and its good ending.*

She considered the war had had a good ending for her friend "Ned". In 1918, Edwin Landseer Lutyens, OM, KCIE, PRA, FRIBA was knighted. A year later, Prime Minister David Lloyd George invited him to build a temporary "catafalque" for the ceremony to be held in Whitehall on the first anniversary of the Armistice, 19th July 1919. Sir Edwin preferred the term "Cenotaph" – "a monument erected to a deceased person whose body is elsewhere." The base soon became swamped with wreaths, and it was decided that a permanent memorial must be erected. This was unveiled by King George V on 11th November 1920. Since then, a Service of Remembrance is held in Whitehall, and in every church in the country, on the Sunday closest to 11th November. Lloyd George wrote to

Lutyens, *"The Cenotaph by its very simplicity fittingly expresses the memory in which the people hold all those who so bravely fought and died for the country."*

However, a respectful resting place was needed for the half-a-million men who had been killed and the numerous "missing". In previous conflicts, a soldier was buried on the spot where he died, and only a commissioned officer was laid in a coffin. This was no longer acceptable to society. It demanded the return of its dead, but with such a number it was impractical. On the west wall of St Mary's Byfleet parish church hang grave markers, rough wooden crosses from the graves of the fallen, which the War Graves Commission later replaced with simple white headstones. Lutyens was amongst the architects who designed the cemeteries *for those who grow not old as we that are left grow old*. The Imperial War Graves Commission asked Miss Jekyll to submit planting schemes. She chose flowers that the young men knew and grew in their gardens, such as white thrift and roses.

On 23rd April 1923, a young bride laid her bouquet at the tomb of the Unknown Soldier. She was the former Lady Elizabeth Bowes-Lyon, and had just married the King's second son, Prince Albert, Duke of York. He proposed three times. She refused him twice because she feared "never again to be free to think, speak and act as I feel I ought to". The young couple spent part of their honeymoon (26th April to 7th May) with Mrs Greville at Polesden Lacey. Presumably, Chef was cajoled into serving the "baby tongues" given only to royalty, and prepared his speciality, "Oeufs Duc", for the Duke.

When the Duchess of York returned from the couple's highly successful state visit to France (1938), she heard that Mrs Greville was unwell. Immediately Elizabeth called into Charles Street, Mrs Greville's London home. The Duchess told of the fabulous time France had given her and how Paris had fallen in love with Hartnell's all-white trousseaux. She told the sick woman about Mlle France and Mlle Marianne, two dolls designed by Jumeau. The French government presented them to the couple as gifts for their two daughters, Princess Elizabeth and Princess Margaret Rose. The toys came with 350 outfits designed by courtiers such as Worth, Lanvin, Cartier, Hermes, and Vuitton. They possessed twenty-two pairs of shoes and fifty-six pairs of gloves, and even owned their own motorcar. Elizabeth chatted away. She knew she was talking to a woman who loved gossip and was fascinated by people.

The Duchess's mother, Lady Strathmore, commented, "Certain people have to be fed Royalty like sea-horses fish." Although Mrs Greville held a political saloon, it was people who pursued careers, made history, or did big things in the arts who really interested her, and it was usually men more than women who fascinated her. She told the author Beverley Nichols, "If I ever had had a daughter I would like her to be like the Duchess of York." He was, like Mrs Greville, a snob, and unlikely to refrain from letting her know that the myrtle in his garden came from a sprig in Queen Victoria's wedding bouquet. However, he was unlikely to mention his predilection for "rough-trade", especially guardsmen. Unlike Mrs Greville, Nichols loved gardens, numbering among his friends Constance Spry, Violet Sackville-West, and President of the RHS Lord Aberconway. One thing Mrs Greville did tell Mr Nichols and many other people: "I plan to leave Polesden Lacey to the dear Duchess of York."

CHAPTER EIGHT

1930–1939

The Final Chapter

Shortly before she died, Miss Jekyll discovered the wireless. It had been introduced to her by Lutyens, who persuaded her to have one. Like Harry, she decided that, after all, "it was a great blessing". In fact, Miss Jekyll preferred to drift into sleep listening to it rather than read a book. However, both elderly people considered it peculiar that voices could come through the air. "Unnatural," they said. However, Miss Jekyll never countenanced using a typewriter, but did tolerate the telephone, which Harry did not.

Throughout her old age, like many people of her generation, Miss Jekyll's routine remained the same, never wavering even when the temperature reached 86.5 degrees Fahrenheit in the shade. Lutyens reported:

8 a.m. called by maid: Florence Hayter
9 to 9.30 a.m. Breakfast:
    included sausages, iced buns, eggs, coffee etc.
                Work in garden or workroom
11 a.m. beef tea
                Work in garden or workroom
Mid-day Luncheon: usually included:
    beef-suet pudding, beer, stuffed- tomatoes.
1 p.m. read newspapers
                        Rest
3 p.m. Work in garden or workroom

4.30 – 5 p.m. Tea

Rest

7.30 p.m. Work in garden or workroom
Followed by a hearty dinner.
11 p.m. and so to bed.

On 8th December 1932, Gertrude Jekyll died. She had written her own epithet: . . . *a garden is a grand teacher. It teaches patience and careful watchfulness; it teaches industry and thrift. . . . The good gardener knows with absolute certainty that if he does his part . . . so surely will God give the increase.*

Just before Christmas 1932, George bought a wireless as well. Harry wished to hear the King speaking "over the airwaves". It must have been uncomfortable for an elderly man to sit in a box room under the stairs of Sandringham House and talk into a microphone. Although the speech was written by Rudyard Kipling, the King spoke directly to his people: "Through the marvels of modern science, I am enabled, this Christmas Day, to speak to all my peoples throughout the Empire." His Majesty stressed his wish to serve and how moved he was by their loyalty and confidence in him. Immediately he heard the King's voice, Harry rose to his feet and stood to attention. Flo snapped: "Whatever are you doing, Pa? Sit down, do."

"I am in the presence of my King," he answered.

"He can't see you."

"How do I know? I can hear *him*."

On 20th January 1936, King George V died. Harry learned of his death with sadness and concern for the old Queen. He sensed she was about to face a terrible dilemma. Miss Jekyll and the Queen were women from the upper classes, expected to be pillars of strength in an ever-changing world, and the families of both women described them as "tomboys".

"Service" was the guiding rule of George V and Queen Mary's lives. It was something Miss Jekyll understood, and Harry expected from "the gentry". Charlie's old Bishop heard a story that as the King's funeral procession began making its way for the lying-in-state, part of the Imperial Crown fell from the top of the coffin, landing in the gutter. "It is a bad omen," Harry said. He had never considered the Prince of Wales to possess the stuff which makes a King. "Lightweight, charm, no backbone," he snapped. He recalled how shocked the Prince had been when he visited Wales. He said to the miners, "Something must be done." Nothing was.

Flo thought of an old photograph. A good-looking little boy sat on his grandmother's knee. Hannah said to her, "He's just the type, Flo, to get caught by the wrong woman." Charlie whispered, "It's all so romantic." George refused to discuss the matter. He picked up his cup. Put it to his lips. Conversation was at an end.

During that year, the *London Illustrated News* commissioned a painting of the new King. It was needed for the special coronation issue. Edward had been the glamorous, popular Prince of Wales whom every girl wished to dance with and longed to marry. But Edward maintained his liking for older, married women, and continued wanting to marry his current lover, the American, twice-married Mrs Wallis Simpson. He would even settle for a morganatic marriage. Prime Minister Stanley Baldwin, the Archbishop of Canterbury Cosmo Lang, the Austrian and Canadian governments, and most of the English establishment refused to countenance such a prospect.

Mrs Simpson was about to dispose of her current husband. She was a provincial American. Many people said, "She is nobody from nowhere." Ordinary women snapped, "Mrs Simpson is no more Royal than I am." Others thought she had Nazi leanings. There were rumours of lovers beside the King, such as an unknown man called Trundle, and Hitler's ambassador to London, Joachim von Ribbentrop. Nevertheless, the overseas press could not get enough of Mrs Simpson, a charismatic figure, pin-thin, in chic black dresses, face as white as her pearls, with vivid red lipstick slashed across her face. Virginia

Woolf said, "Mrs Simpson dresses well but the Duchess has the kinder heart." The King's mistress nicknamed the Duchess of York "Cookie". Her English paisley charm could not compete with the American woman's hard-edged sharpness. The country and the world waited for Edward to come to a decision on whether to rule alone or marry and go.

All through the affair, the English press remained discreet on the "King's Great Matter". Only towards the end did people like Harry learn about the crisis facing the country and the empire. The future of the Royal family itself was in jeopardy. Virginia Woolf talked of crowds "waiting in the cold, watching two or three lights burning in the upper windows of Buckingham Palace". As the King dithered, so public sympathy began to wane.

Flo devoured the *Daily Express*, Charlie listened to the wireless, and Harry prayed. He heard that Lord Onslow took the view that the Victorian age was over and the King should marry whom he pleased, but many thought Mrs Simpson had no real love for the King and was beginning to want to be free of him.

Finally, the King made his decision. On 10th December 1936, Edward VIII, in the presence of his brothers the Dukes of York, Kent, and Gloucester, signed the instrument of abdication at his private residence, Fort Belvedere. The next day, the Duke of York, a nervous, delicate man with a stammer, wept on his mother's shoulder and made up his mind to become good King George VI.

On 11th December 1936, Harry, George, Flo, and Charlie sat in silence as the ex-King's voice came over the airwaves. Harry did not rise to his feet. Mrs Simpson had tried to persuade the King to talk directly to his people and explain his problems. Edward began: "At last I am able to say a few words of my own. I have never wanted to withhold anything, but until now it has not been constitutionally possible for me to speak. A few hours ago I discharged my last duty as King and Emperor, and now that I have been succeeded by my brother, the Duke of York, my first words must be to declare my allegiance to him. This I do with all my heart. . . ." He finished the speech with "and now, we all have a new King. I wish him and you, his people, happiness and prosperity with all my heart. God bless you all. God save the King!"

The *London Illustrated News* cancelled the special edition. The next day, the American newspapers shrieked "Edward Gone, George King" as the Duke of York was proclaimed King George VI. The English headlines announced, "Prince Edward, Duke of Windsor, arrived late last night at the Schloss Enzersfeld," a lonely castle in the Austrian mountains near Vienna. He had reigned for ten months and twenty-one days.

Like Harry, Mrs Greville did not consider the Prince of Wales suitable material for kingship, but she complained, "I was so happy in the days when they used to run in and out of the house as if they were my own children." However, the Royal couple kept their friendship with Mrs Greville, but they lived in a different world from "Tum-Tum's" (Edward VII, the King's indulgent grandfather). George VI enjoyed spending his evenings with his stamp collection while the Queen sat quietly knitting socks.

On 3rd May 1937, Mrs Simpson's divorce degree became absolute. On 3rd June 1937, the Duke of Windsor made her his wife. The Royal family would not allow the Duchess to be called "Your Royal Highness". She was to be addressed as "Your Grace" – a term used for non-royal dukes and duchesses. On 27th March 1970, the *BBC* interviewed the Windsors. The Duchess said she thought she may have enjoyed running an advertising agency.

On 12th May 1937, the same day that was planned for Edward VIII's coronation, George VI was crowned instead. Harry walked to Granny Powell's to listen to the ceremony on her wireless. Charlie drove Flo and George to offices in Whitehall where a RHS committee member had invited them to watch the coronation procession.

They saw the carriages and horses pass slowly under their windows, going at walking pace. Eight white horses pulled the King and Queen's gold state coach. The King looked "grave, white and lean". George saw "his lady". She was dignified and serious. In another carriage, the heir to the throne, eleven-year-old Princess Elizabeth, clutched her coronet, trying not to look excited. Her sister, seven-year-old Princess Margaret Rose, did not even try. Elizabeth described the journey to the Abbey as "jolty".

The group in the Whitehall offices listened to the service on the wireless while watching the crowds below. The commentator did not mention when the Dean of Westminster, Dr Christopher Foxley-Norris, fell down some steps while carrying St Edward's crown. It only survived because of the ribbons attached to the cushion. They did not hear Princess Elizabeth whisper "there is a wonder as Papa is crowned." She then became bored. When the service was over, she wrote *"Finis"* firmly on her programme. The six-mile-long procession returned to the Palace. King George complained, "I never had such an uncomfortable journey in my life."

At 4 p.m., amidst a sudden downpour, George, Flo, and Charlie started on their journey back to Wisley. They heard later that it was not until 9 p.m. that the last person left the Abbey. After she became Queen, George did not chat casually to "his lady" again. However, when they were old people, they did meet again. On 28th July 1954, HM Queen Elizabeth The Queen Mother came to open Aberconway House. She was escorted by her brother, David Bowes-Lyon, the RHS President. The hostel overlooks Seven Acres Fields and provides accommodation and a study centre for the Society's students. Horticulture remains one of the country's foremost employers, and the RHS prepares students for roles from hands-on gardeners to research scientists.

Early in the afternoon, George put on his black jacket and striped trousers and prepared to receive from "his lady" a gold watch, a reward for fifty years of loyal service. By this time,

George was becoming slightly deaf. When he arrived on the rostrum, he leant forward and put his hand behind his ear: "What was that, Ma'am?"

"I said Mr Hilderley," the Queen replied gently.

When the ceremony was over, the waiting reporters asked him, "What did she say?" "What do you think of her?" He replied, "She's a nice gal, a very nice gal indeed." He picked up his cup, put it to his lips, conversation at an end.

Ted, the youngest of Granny Powell's charges, watched the coronation procession on a flickering nine-inch television set in Miss Vera Georgina Kilford's sitting room in Cobham. "We don't have a parlour, Ted," she said. Vera was a small, sharp, well-dressed young woman, born in Paddington, and a great admirer of Mrs Simpson's style. She was the fashion buyer in charge of Ladies Clothing for Gamages department store in Cobham High Street. It also sold gentleman's clothing and household items, but that was no concern of Miss Kilford's. She asked her juniors to "Step forward, Miss . . . ," and enquired "Are you free, Miss . . . ?" Payment was placed in a tube which was then whisked overhead into the account clerk's office.

Miss Kilford dressed the windows with Gor-Ray permanent pleated skirts, matching twinsets, and Jaeger summer frocks. At Christmas time, only one item was displayed – a long silk dress, a copy of a French couture design, no price given. In a discreet room off the main shop, Miss Kilford sold foundation garments and silk and lisle stockings together with suspender belts. There were drawers full of Simple, Vogue, and McCall dress-making patterns together with knitting patterns. Displayed on a counter was an afternoon blouse "knitted for glamour": *This gives a sophisticated effect with its little bow. It needs just 12 oz cotton boucle or rayon boucle, 2 No. 12 knitting pins and 5 buttons and press-studs. It fits a size 34 bust.* Miss Kilford neither knitted nor wore it.

Ted owned a motorbike which Miss Kilford scorned. She travelled up and down the Portsmouth Road in her little Austin

Seven. Marge made a note of Ted's girlfriends. Vera was number thirty-three. She was the only one who introduced him to the crowd at the Hut. On 8th September 1936, Marge and Charlie married. She told Ted that "Vera Kilford is flighty, she will never marry you."

On 5th September 1939, Ted and Vera married. The *Surrey Advertiser* wrote of *'Miss Kilford's pretty wedding'*. It took place in the small Victorian chapel belonging to Hatchford Park. The young couple did not go on honeymoon to Switzerland as planned because, at 11 a.m. on 3rd September 1939, Prime Minister Chamberlain announced "the country is at war." Granny Powell and Harry were not at Ted and Vera's wedding. They had died during the earlier months of the year. Harry did not have to live through another War. This time, it was Ted and Charlie who went away.

When a bomb landed close to Polesden Lacey, Mrs Greville said, "I told Ribbentrop, he might beat the English, but he will never beat the Scots." In 1942, she died. The politician Sir John Simon, who had proposed to her, said, "I find it poignant that there is no one – neither husband, nor child, nor brother nor sister to whom to send a message of sympathy and condolence." Mrs Greville had told her friends, "Most people leave their money to the poor. I'm leaving mine to the rich." Princess Margaret received £20,000, and Queen Elizabeth received a diamond necklace reputedly once belonging to Marie Antoinette, and emeralds, formerly the property of Empress Josephine, together with diamond chandelier earrings and a tiara by Boucheron.

Polesden Lacey? Mrs Greville left that to the National Trust.

In 1945, the 5th Earl of Onslow died. In 1956, the Countess of Iveagh bought Clandon Park from her nephew, the 6th Earl, and presented it to the National Trust, "thus saving my home from an uncertain future".

Sutton Place remains in private hands. In 1959, Paul Getty, the American oil magnate, bought the estate from the Duke of

Sutherland. Occasionally, Ripley saw the reclusive Mr Getty driving through the village in his battered Cadillac.

Flo and George remained at 5 The Square. On 18th February 1939, George wrote in the Great Bible, "Today Harry Worsfold (1839–1939) died. He said he was the last of the Parish Constables. He was certainly the last of a breed of men." George closed the book. It was never written in again.

There is a postscript to this story. One night, Harry's great-granddaughter woke in the little box-like bedroom. It was utterly cold, deeply dark, silent, and quite still, as it can only be in the country. She dare not open her eyes. The next morning, she told her grandparents. "Nasty dream," they said. Ten years later, her grandmother told her "that was the night Great-Grandfather died." So she did as he wished; she wrote his story. You are reading it now.